Hoisting and Rigging
Safety Manual

Infrastructure Health & Safety Association

21 Voyager Court South
Etobicoke, Ontario M9W 5M7 Canada
1-800-263-5024
info@ihsa.ca   www.ihsa.ca

Disclaimer

The contents contained in this publication are for general information only. This publication should not be regarded or relied upon as a definitive guide to government regulations or to safety practices and procedures. The contents of this publication were, to the best of our knowledge, current at the time of printing. However, no representations of any kind are made with regard to the accuracy, completeness, or sufficiency of the contents. The appropriate regulations and statutes should be consulted. Readers should not act on the information contained herein without seeking specific independent legal advice on their specific circumstance. The Infrastructure Health & Safety Association is pleased to answer individual requests for counselling and advice.

© Infrastructure Health and Safety Association, 1995

Revised, May 1997
Revised, April 2001
Revised, January 2007
Revised, September 2008
Revised, September 2009
Second printing, August 2010
Third printing, August 2011
Fourth printing, March 2012
Fifth printing, June 2018
Sixth printing, January 2020

ISBN-13: 978-0-919465-70-1

TABLE of CONTENTS

INTRODUCTION

Purpose of this Manual

This manual is intended as a working guide for training workers and supervisors in the fundamentals of safe rigging and hoisting.

The information covers not only ropes and knots but hoisting equipment from cranes to chainfalls and rigging hardware from rope clips to spreader beams. Equally important is the attention paid at every point to correct procedures for inspection, maintenance, and operation.

Knowledge of the equipment and materials with which we work is one of the most important factors in occupational health and safety. Each item has been designed and developed to serve a specific purpose. Recognizing its capabilities and limitations not only improves efficiency but minimizes hazards and helps prevent accidents.

This manual identifies the basic hazards in rigging and hoisting, explains the safeguards necessary to control or eliminate these hazards, and spells out other essential safety requirements.

The information should be used in conjunction with the applicable regulations by contractors, supervisors, operators, riggers, and others delivering or receiving instruction in the basics of safe rigging and hoisting.

Health and Safety Law

Occupational Health and Safety Act

Safety legislation for Ontario construction in general consists of the *Occupational Health and Safety Act*, which came into force on 1 October 1979. Its purpose is to protect workers against health and safety hazards on the job.

The *Occupational Health and Safety Act* is based on the "internal responsibility" concept for management and workers. This encourages both groups to work out solutions to health and safety problems with the guidance of the Ministry of Labour.

The Act provides us with the framework and the tools to achieve a safe and healthy workplace. It sets out the rights and duties of all parties in the workplace. It establishes procedures for dealing with job-site hazards and provides for enforcement of the law where compliance has not been achieved voluntarily.

Over the years the *Act* has been revised to meet the changing requirements of Ontario's workplaces.

Regulations

There are various regulations under the Act for construction in particular.

The most extensive is the Construction Regulation (Ontario Regulation 213/91). There are also special regulations for controlled products under the Workplace Hazardous Materials Information System (WHMIS) and for designated substances such as asbestos.

Construction regulations are generally based on health and safety problems that have recurred over the years. In many cases, the regulations have been proposed jointly by management and labour groups as a means of controlling or eliminating problems that have historically resulted in fatalities, lost-time injuries, and occupational diseases.

The Construction Regulation has been periodically revised over the years.

Review Ontario's *Occupational Health and Safety Act,* the Construction Regulation, and other applicable health and safety regulations to make sure that you know what to expect from others on the job – and what others expect from you.

Hoisting and Rigging Hazards

- Procedures and Precautions
- Determining Load Weights
- Weights of Common Materials

Section 1

Hoisting and Rigging Hazards

It is important that workers involved with hoisting and rigging activities are trained in both safety and operating procedures. Hoisting equipment should be operated only by trained personnel.

The cause of rigging accidents can often be traced to a lack of knowledge on the part of a rigger. Training programs such as the Infrastructure Health & Safety Association's *Basic Safety Training for Hoisting and Rigging* provide workers with a basic knowledge of principles relating to safe hoisting and rigging practices in the construction industry.

A safe rigging operation requires the rigger to know

- the weight of the load and rigging hardware
- the capacity of the hoisting device
- the working load limit of the hoisting rope, slings, and hardware.

When the weights and capacities are known, the rigger must then determine how to lift the load so that it is stable.

Training and experience enable riggers to recognize hazards that can have an impact on a hoisting operation. Riggers must be aware of elements that can affect hoisting safety, factors that reduce capacity, and safe practices in rigging, lifting, and landing loads. Riggers must also be familiar with the proper inspection and use of slings and other rigging hardware.

Most crane and rigging accidents can be prevented by field personnel following basic safe hoisting and rigging practices. When a crane operator is working with a rigger or a rigging crew, it is vital that the operator is aware of the all aspects of the lift and that a means of communication has been agreed upon, including what signals will be used.

Elements that can Affect Hoisting Safety

- **Working Load Limit (WLL) not known.** Don't assume. Know the working load limits of the equipment being used. Never exceed these limits.

- **Defective components.** Examine all hardware, tackle, and slings before use. Destroy defective components. Defective equipment that is merely discarded may be picked up and used by someone unaware of its defects.

- **Questionable equipment.** Do not use equipment that is suspected to be unsafe or unsuitable, until its suitability has been verified by a competent person.

- **Hazardous wind conditions.** Never carry out a hoisting or rigging operation when winds create hazards for workers, the general public, or property. Assess load size and shape to determine whether wind conditions may cause problems. For example, even though the weight of the load may be within the capacity of the equipment, loads with large wind-catching surfaces may swing or rotate out of control during the lift in high or gusting winds. Swinging and rotating loads not only present a danger to riggers—there is the potential for the forces to overload the hoisting equipment.

- **Weather conditions.** When the visibility of riggers or hoist crew is impaired by snow, fog, rain, darkness, or dust, extra caution must be exercised. For example, operate in "all slow", and if necessary, the lift should be postponed. At sub-freezing temperatures, be aware that loads are likely to be frozen to the ground or structure they are resting on. In extreme cold conditions avoid shock-loading or impacting the hoist equipment and hardware, which may have become brittle.

- **Electrical contact.** One of the most frequent killers of riggers is electrocution. An electrical path can be created when a part of the hoist, load line, or load comes into close proximity to an energized overhead powerline. When a crane is operating near a live powerline and the load, hoist lines, or any other part of the hoisting operation could encroach on the minimum permitted distance (see table on the next page), specific measures described in the Construction Regulation must be taken. For example, constructors must have written procedures to prevent contact whenever equipment operates within the minimum permitted distance from a live overhead powerline. The constructor must have copies of the procedure available for every employer on the project.

- **Hoist line not plumb.** The working load limits of hoisting equipment apply only to freely suspended loads on plumb hoist lines. If the hoist line is not plumb during load handling, side loads are created which can destabilize the equipment and cause structural failure or tip-over, with little warning.

Wrong. The hoist line must be plumb at all times.

Keep the Minimum Distance from Powerlines

Normal phase-to-phase voltage rating	Minimum distance
750 or more volts, but no more than 150,000 volts	3 metres
Over 150,000 volts, but no more than 250,000 volts	4.5 metres
More than 250,000 volts	6 metres

Beware:
The wind can blow powerlines, hoist lines, or your load.
This can cause them to cross the minimum distance.

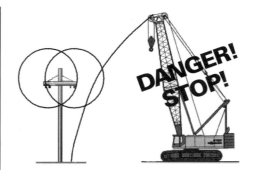

This crane boom could reach within the minimum distance.

Factors that Reduce Capacity

The working load limits of hoisting and rigging equipment are based on ideal conditions. Such ideal circumstances are seldom achieved in the field. Riggers must therefore recognize the factors that can reduce the capacity of the hoist.

– **Swing.** The swinging of suspended loads creates additional dynamic forces on the hoist in addition to the weight of the load. The additional dynamic forces (see point below) are difficult to quantify and account for, and could cause tip-over of the crane or failure of hoisting hardware. The force of the swinging action makes the load drift away from the machine, increasing the radius and side-loading on the equipment. The load should be kept directly below the boom point or upper load block. This is best accomplished by controlling the load's movement with slow motions.

– **Condition of equipment.** The rated working load limits apply only to equipment and hardware in good condition. Any equipment damaged in service should be taken out of service and repaired or destroyed.

– **Dynamic forces.** The working load limits of rigging and hoisting equipment are determined for static loads. The design safety factor is applied to account, in part, for the dynamic motions of the load and equipment. To ensure that the working load limit is not exceeded during operation, allow for wind loading and other dynamic forces created by the movements of the machine and its load. Avoid sudden snatching, swinging, and stopping of suspended loads. Rapid acceleration and deceleration also increases these dynamic forces.

– **Weight of tackle.** The rated load of hoisting equipment does not account for the weight of hook blocks, hooks, slings, equalizer beams, and other parts of the lifting tackle. The combined weight of these items must be added to the total weight of the load, and the capacity of the hoisting equipment, including design safety factors, must be large enough to account for the extra load to be lifted.

Slings

After the hoist rope, the sling is the most commonly used piece of rigging equipment. Observe the following precautions with slings.

- Never use damaged slings. Inspect slings regularly to ensure their safety. Check wire rope slings for kinking, wear, abrasion, broken wires, worn or cracked fittings, loose seizings and splices, crushing, flattening, and rust or corrosion. Pay special attention to the areas around thimbles and other fittings.

- Slings should be marked with an identification number and their maximum capacity on a flat ferrule or permanently attached ring. Mark the capacity of the sling for a vertical load or at an angle of 45°. Ensure that everyone is aware of how the rating system works.

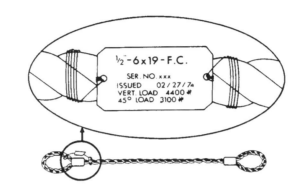

- Avoid sharp bends, pinching, and crushing. Use loops and thimbles at all times. Corner pads that prevent the sling from being sharply bent or cut can be made from split sections of large-diameter pipe, corner saddles, padding, or blocking.

Ensure that Slings are Protected at All Sharp Corners on Heavy Items

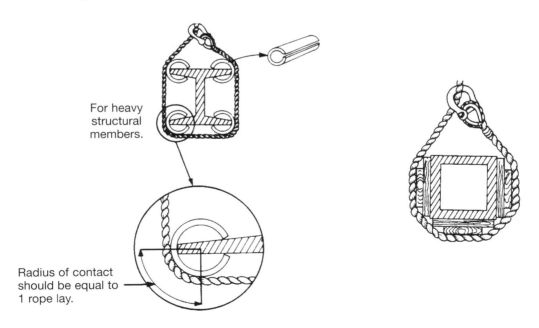

For heavy structural members.

Radius of contact should be equal to 1 rope lay.

- Never allow wire rope slings, or any wire rope, to lie on the ground for long periods of time or on damp or wet surfaces, rusty steel, or near corrosive substances.
- Avoid dragging slings out from underneath loads.
- Keep wire rope slings away from flame cutting and electric welding.
- Never make slings from discarded hoist rope.
- Avoid using single-leg wire rope slings with hand-spliced eyes. The load can spin, causing the rope to unlay and the splice to pull out. Use slings with Flemish Spliced Eyes.

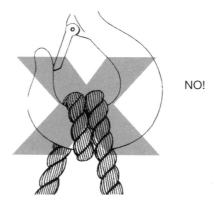

Never Wrap a Sling Around a Hook

- Never wrap a wire sling completely around a hook. The sharp radius will damage the sling. Use the eye.

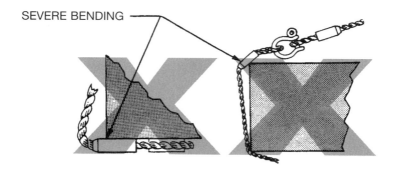

Do Not Permit Bending Near Any Splice or Attached Fitting

- Avoid bending the eye section of wire rope slings around corners. The bend will weaken the splice or swaging. There must be no bending near any attached fitting.

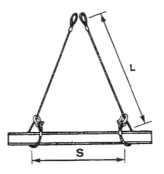

If L is greater than S then sling angle is OK.

Check on Sling Angle

- Ensure that the sling angle is always greater than 45° and preferably greater than 60°. When the horizontal distance between the attachment points on the load is less than the length of the shortest sling leg, then the angle is greater than 60° and generally safe.

- **Multi-leg slings.** With slings having more than two legs and a rigid load, it is possible for some of the legs to take practically the full load while the others merely balance it. There is no way of knowing that each leg is carrying its fair share of the load.

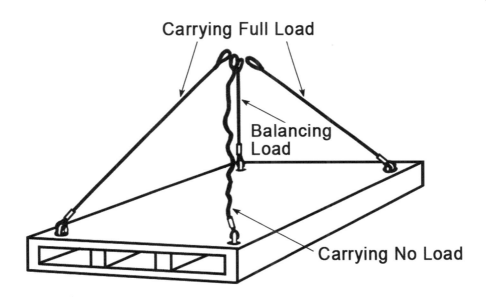

As a result, when lifting rigid objects with three- or four-leg bridle slings, make sure that at least two of the legs alone can support the total load. In other words, consider multi-leg slings used on a rigid load as having only two legs.

When using multi-leg slings to lift loads in which one end is much heavier than the other (i.e., some legs simply provide balance), the tension on the most heavily loaded leg(s) is more important than the tension on the more lightly loaded legs. In these situations, slings are selected to support the most heavily loaded leg(s). Do not treat each leg as equally loaded (i.e., do not divide the total weight by the number of legs.) Keep in mind that the motion of the load during hoisting and travel can cause the weight to shift into different legs. This will result in increases and decreases on the load of any leg.

- When using choker hitches, forcing the eye down towards the load increases tension in the sling, which can result in rope damage. Use thimbles and shackles to reduce friction on the running line.

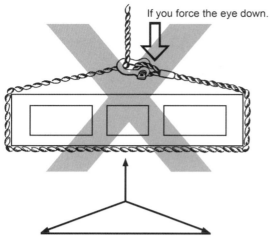

If you force the eye down.

Low sling angles create severe loading on the sling.

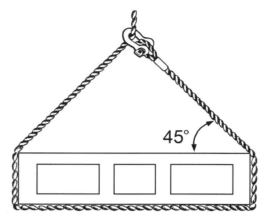

45°

Let the eye ride higher and keep this angle approx. 45° or more.

Incorrect – Cutting action of eye splice on running line.

Correct – Use thimbles in the eyes.

Incorrect – Shackle pin bearing on running line can work loose.

Correct – Shackle pin cannot turn.

- Whenever two or more rope eyes must be placed over a hook, install a shackle on the hook with the shackle pin resting in the hook and attach the rope eyes to the shackle. This will prevent the spread of the sling legs from opening up the hook and prevent the eyes from damaging each other under load.

Whenever 2 or more ropes are to be Placed Over a Hook – Use a Shackle

Rigging, Lifting, and Landing Loads

- Rig loads to prevent any parts from shifting or dislodging during the lift. Suspended loads should be securely slung and properly balanced before they are set in motion.
- Keep the load under control at all times. Use one or more taglines to prevent uncontrolled motion.

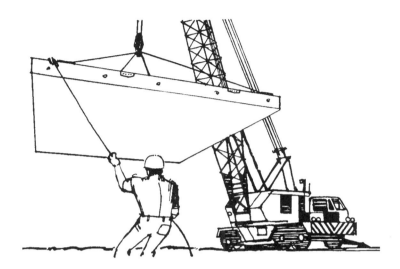

Use Tag Lines to Control All Loads

- Loads must be safely landed and properly blocked before being unhooked and unslung.
- Lifting beams should be plainly marked with their weight and designed working loads, and should only be used for their intended purpose.
- Never wrap the hoist rope around the load. Attach the load to only the hook, with slings or other rigging devices.
- The load line should be brought over the load's centre of gravity before the lift is started.
- Keep hands away from pinch points as slack is being taken up.
- Wear gloves when handling wire rope.
- Make sure that everyone stands clear when loads are being lifted, lowered, and freed of slings. As slings are being withdrawn, they may catch under the load and suddenly fly loose.

- Before making a lift, check to see that the sling is properly attached to the load.
- Never work under a suspended load.
- Never make temporary repairs to a sling. Procedures for proper repair should be established and followed.
- Secure or remove unused sling legs of a multi-leg sling before the load is lifted.

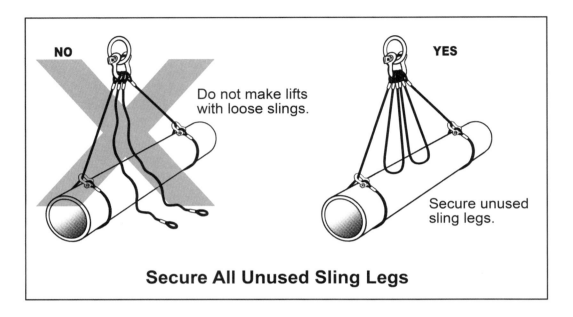

NO

Do not make lifts with loose slings.

YES

Secure unused sling legs.

Secure All Unused Sling Legs

- Never point-load a hook unless it is designed and rated for such use.
- Begin a lift by raising the load slightly to make sure that the load is free and that all sling legs are taking the load.
- Avoid impact loading caused by sudden jerking during lifting and lowering. Take up slack on the sling gradually. Avoid lifting or swinging the load over workers below.
- When using two or more slings on a load, ensure that they are all made from the same material.
- Prepare adequate blocking before loads are lowered. Blocking can help prevent damage to slings.

Determining Load Weights

A key step in rigging is determining the weight of the load that will be hoisted.

You can obtain the load's weight from shipping papers, design plans, catalogue data, manufacturer's specifications, and other dependable sources. On erection plans, the size of steel beams is usually provided along with their weight and length. If weight information is not provided, you will have to calculate it.

Calculating weight

You can calculate the approximate weight of a steel object using a standard weight and applying the formulas for area and volume. The standard weight for steel is: 1 square foot of steel an inch thick will weigh about 40 pounds.

Applying that standard weight for steel to calculate the weight of two steel plates measuring 1 1/2" x 3' x 6' results in the following:

2 (sheets) x 1.5" (thickness) x 3' x 6' (area) x 40 lb (weight per square foot, 1" thick) = 2160 pounds.
[2 x 1.5 x 3 x 6 x 40 = 2160 pounds]

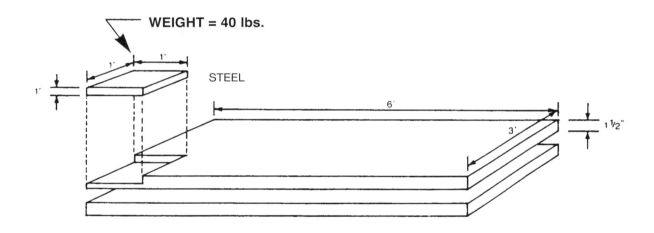

Calculating the weight of various shapes of steel

To estimate the weight of various shapes of steel, it helps to envision the steel object as a flat plate—visually separate the parts, or imagine flattening them into rectangles.

Angle iron has a structural shape that can be considered a bent plate. If you flattened the angle iron, the result is a plate. For example, 5 x 3 x 1/4-inch angle iron would flatten out to approximately a 1/4-inch plate that is 8 inches wide.

Once you have figured out the flattened size, the volume and weight can be calculated like we did in the previous section. Since the calculations for the standard weight of steel is expressed in square feet per inch thickness, the 8-inch width must be divided by 12 to get the fraction of a foot that it represents. The 1/4" thickness is already expressed as a fraction of one inch. In this case, the angle iron weighs approximately 6.67 pounds (40 lb x 8" ÷ 12" x 1/4" = 6.67). Multiply this weight by the length (in feet) to get the total weight.

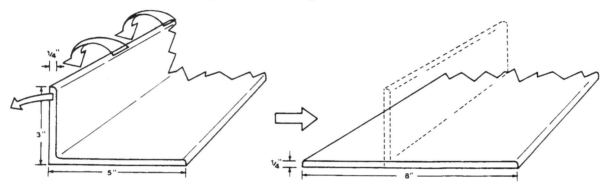

Plates are often rolled into tanks or other shapes. In order to calculate the weight of a circular or spherical piece of steel, first you need to determine the square foot area. To determine the square foot area, you have to figure out the circumference (the distance around the edge of the circle) and the area. To get the circumference of a circle, multiply the diameter by 3.14.

A stack 6 ft. in diameter would have a circumference of 6 ft. x 3.14, or 18.84 ft. To compute the weight of this stack, if it were 30 ft. high and made of 3/8 in. plate, mentally unroll it and flatten it out (Fig. 1.1). This gives a plate 18.84 ft. wide by 30 ft. long by 3/8" thick. The weight is:
$$18.84 \times 30 \times 3/8 \times 40 = 8{,}478 \text{ lbs.}$$

The following formula gives the area of circular objects.

radius (r) = diameter divided by 2
area = πr^2 (π = 3.14)

$$\text{AREA} = 3.14 \times \frac{\text{diameter}}{2} \times \frac{\text{diameter}}{2}$$

Thus, if the stack had an end cap 3/8" thick and 6 ft. in diameter (see Fig. 1.2), it would have a surface area:

AREA = 3.14 x 6/2 x 6/2 = 28.3 sq. ft.

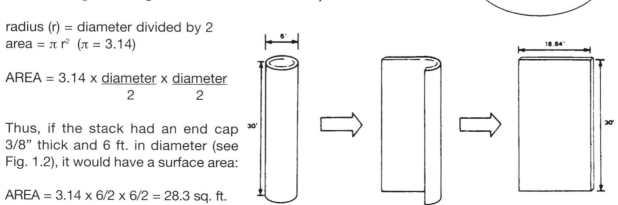

and would weigh: 28.3 x 3/8 x 40 = 425 lbs. (Figure 1.2)

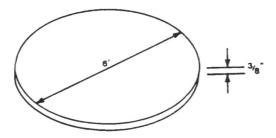

Load Weight Determination
Figure 1.2

For other materials the weights are normally based on their weight per cubic foot, so you have to determine how many cubic feet of material (the volume) you are hoisting in order to estimate the weight.

For example, suppose you have a bundle of spruce lumber to hoist and the bundle is 12 ft. long, 3' high and 4' wide. (Fig. 1.3) The weight per cubic foot from Table 1.2 is 28 lbs., so the weight of this bundle is 12 x 3 x 4 x 28 = 4,032 lbs.

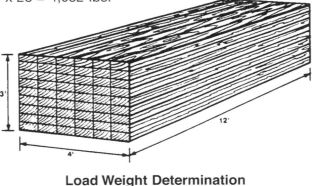

Load Weight Determination
Figure 1.3

The time taken to calculate the approximate weight of any object, whether steel, plates, columns, girders, castings, bedplates, etc., is time well spent and may save a serious accident through failure of lifting gear. The following tables of weights of various materials (Tables 1.1, 1.2, 1.3) should enable any rigger to compute the approximate weight of a given load. When in doubt, do not lift the load. Seek assistance from others who know, or can help determine, the load's weight.

In hoisting and rigging applications, sometimes you will need to account for resistive forces. One example is when hoist lines are being used over pulleys to change the direction of the hoist line. Another example is when loads are being pulled along a surface. Pulleys and rollers on the ground will add some resistance that must be included in load calculations.

Calculating pull required

Horizontal moves require relatively little force to move. Generally, the force to move the load on a smooth, clean and flat surface, using rollers in excellent condition will be about 5% of the load weight. This is roughly the force required to overcome friction and start the load moving. To calculate the amount of pull you need to move up an incline, use the following method.

Caution:
Though widely used because of its simplicity, this method provides an approximate value that is higher than the actual force required. The formula is more accurate for slight inclines (1:5) than steep inclines (1:1). Table 1 shows the difference between the actual pull required and the pull calculated. This simplified method is adequate for most applications. You may need more accurate calculations for large loads.

Table 1

Force Calculated by Simplified Method vs. Actual Force	
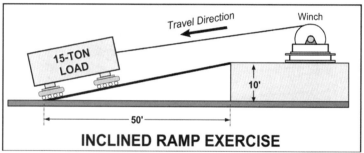	Simplified Method F = .250 W Actual Force F = .245 W Error 2%
	Simplified Method F = .383 W Actual Force F = .364 W Error 5%
	Simplified Method F = .550 W Actual Force F = .492 W Error 12%
	Simplified Method F = 1.05 W Actual Force F = .742 W Error 42%

Exercise

Calculate the force of the load in the following situation. A 15-ton compressor is to be lowered 10 feet. A ramp has been built with a horizontal run of 50 feet.

INCLINED RAMP EXERCISE

Note: For illustration purposes, a second means of restraint has been omitted.

Formula

F (total force) = W x H ÷ L (lift force) + .05W (horizontal force or resistance)

F = Force that the winch must overcome, H = Height, L = Length,
W = Weight of Load

The slope of the ramp is 10 divided by 50 or 1/5th; so the force required is then 15 tons times 1/5th, plus 5% of 15 tons to allow for friction.

This is equal to 3 tons plus .75 tons. Therefore the required pull is 3.75 tons.

With a winch, use its rated capacity for vertical lifting rather than its horizontal capacity so that you maintain an adequate margin of safety.

Table 2 lists some examples of coefficients of friction. Note that some of the combinations of materials have a considerable range of values.

Table 2

Examples of Friction Coefficients	
Steel on Steel	40 – 60%
Leather on Metal	60%
Wood on Stone	40%
Iron on Stone	30 – 70%
Grease Plates	15%
Load on Wheels or Rollers	2 – 5%

Table 1.1 – APPROXIMATE WEIGHT PER FOOT OF LENGTH OF ROUND STEEL BARS AND RODS

Diameter (inches)	Weight (Lbs.) Per Ft. of Length	Diameter (inches)	Weight (Lbs.) Per Ft. of Length
3/16	.094	1 3/8	5.05
1/4	.167	1 1/2	6.01
5/16	.261	1 5/8	7.05
3/8	.376	1 3/4	8.18
7/16	.511	1 7/8	9.39
1/2	.668	2	10.68
9/16	.845	2 1/8	12.06
5/8	1.04	2 1/4	13.52
3/4	1.50	2 3/8	15.06
7/8	2.04	2 1/2	16.69
1	2.67	2 5/8	18.40
1 1/8	3.38	2 3/4	20.20
1 3/16	3.77	2 7/8	22.07
1 1/4	4.17	3	24.03

Table 1.2 – WEIGHTS OF MATERIAL (Based on Volume)

Material	Approximate Weight Lbs. Per Cubic Foot	Material	Approximate Weight Lbs. Per Cubic Foot
METALS		**TIMBER, AIR-DRY**	
Aluminum	165	Cedar	22
Brass	535	Fir, Douglas, seasoned	34
Bronze	500	Fir, Douglas, unseasoned	40
Copper	560	Fir, Douglas, wet	50
Iron	480	Fir, Douglas, glue laminated	34
Lead	710	Hemlock	30
Steel	490	Pine	30
Tin	460	Poplar	30
MASONRY		Spruce	28
Ashlar masonry	140-160	**LIQUIDS**	
Brick masonry, soft	110	Alcohol, pure	49
Brick masonry, common (about		Gasoline	42
3 tons per thousand)	125	Oils	58
Brick masonry, pressed	140	Water	62
Clay tile masonry, average	60	**EARTH**	
Rubble masonry	130-155	Earth, wet	100
Concrete, cinder, haydite	100-110	Earth, dry (about 2050 lbs.	
Concrete, slag	130	per cu. yd.)	75
Concrete, stone	144	Sand and gravel, wet	120
Concrete, stone, reinforced		Sand and gravel, dry	105
(4050 lbs. per cu. yd.)	150	River sand (about 3240 lbs.	
ICE AND SNOW		per cu. yd.)	120
Ice	56	**VARIOUS BUILDING**	
Snow, dry, fresh fallen	8	**MATERIALS**	
Snow, dry, packed	12-25	Cement, portland, loose	94
Snow, wet	27-40	Cement, portland, set	183
MISCELLANEOUS		Lime, gypsum, loose	53-64
Asphalt	80	Mortar, cement-lime, set	103
Tar	75	Crushed rock (about 2565 lbs	
Glass	160	per cu. yd.)	90-110
Paper	60		

Table 1.3 – WEIGHTS OF MATERIALS (Based on Surface Area)

Material	Approximate Weight Lbs. Per Square Foot	Material	Approximate Weight Lbs. Per Square Foot
CEILINGS		**FLOORING**	
(Per Inch of Thickness)		(Per Inch of Thickness)	
Plaster board	5	Hardwood	5
Acoustic and fire resistive tile	2	Sheathing	2.5
Plaster, gypsum-sand	8	Plywood, fir	3
Plaster, light aggregate	4	Wood block, treated	4
Plaster, cement sand	12	Concrete, finish or fill	12
ROOFING		Mastic base	12
Three-ply felt and gravel	5.5	Mortar base	10
Five-ply felt and gravel	6.5	Terrazzo	12.5
Three-ply felt, no gravel	3	Tile, vinyl inch	1.5
Five-ply felt, no gravel	4	Tile, linoleum 3/16 inch	1
Shingles, wood	2	Tile, cork, per 1/16 inch	0.5
Shingles, asbestos	3	Tile, rubber or asphalt 3/16 inch	2
Shingles, asphalt	2.5	Tile, ceramic or quarry 3/4 inch	11
Shingles, ¼ inch slate	10	Carpeting	2
Shingles, tile	14	**DECKS AND SLABS**	
PARTITIONS		Steel roof deck 1 1/2" – 14 ga.	5
Steel partitions	4	– 16 ga.	4
Solid 2" gypsum-sand plaster	20	– 18 ga.	3
Solid 2" gypsum-light agg. plaster	12	– 20 ga.	2.5
Metal studs, metal lath, 3/4"		– 22 ga.	2
plaster both sides	18	Steel cellular deck 1 1/2" – 12/12 ga.	11
Metal or wood studs, plaster		– 14/14 ga.	8
board and 1/2" plaster both sides	18	– 16/16 ga.	6.5
Plaster 1/2"	4	– 18/18 ga.	5
Hollow clay tile 2 inch	13	– 20/20 ga.	3.5
3 inch	16	Steel cellular deck 3" – 12/12 ga.	12.5
4 inch	18	– 14/14 ga.	9.5
5 inch	20	– 16/16 ga.	7.5
6 inch	25	– 18/18 ga.	6
Hollow slag concrete block 4 inch	24	– 20/20 ga.	4.5
6 inch	35	Concrete, reinforced, per inch	12.5
Hollow gypsum block 3 inch	10	Concrete, gypsum, per inch	5
4 inch	13	Concrete, lightweight, per inch	5-10
5 inch	15.5	**MISCELLANEOUS**	
6 inch	16.5	Windows, glass, frame	8
Solid gypsum block 2 inch	9.5	Skylight, glass, frame	12
3 inch	13	Corrugated asbestos 1/4 inch	3.5
MASONRY WALLS		Glass, plate 1/4 inch	3.5
(Per 4 Inch of Thickness)		Glass, common	1.5
Brick	40	Plastic sheet 1/4 inch	1.5
Glass brick	20	Corrugated steel sheet, galv. – 12 ga.	5.5
Hollow concrete block	30	– 14 ga.	4
Hollow slag concrete block	24	– 16 ga.	3
Hollow cinder concrete block	20	– 18 ga.	2.5
Hollow haydite block	22	– 20 ga.	2
Stone, average	55	– 22 ga.	1.5
Bearing hollow clay tile	23	Wood Joists – 16" ctrs. 2 x 12	3.5
		2 x 10	3
		2 x 8	2.5
		Steel plate (per inch of thickness)	40

Section 2

Fibre Ropes, Knots, Hitches

- **Fibre Rope Characteristics**
- **Inspection of Fibre Rope**
- **Working Load Limit (WLL)**
- **Care, Storage, Use**
- **Knots**
- **Hitches**

Section 2

Fibre Ropes, Knots, Hitches

Fibre rope is a commonly used tool which has many applications in daily hoisting and rigging operations.

Readily available in a wide variety of synthetic and natural fibre materials, these ropes may be used as

- slings for hoisting materials
- handlines for lifting light loads
- taglines for helping to guide and control loads.

There are countless situations where the rigger will be required to tie a safe and reliable knot or hitch in a fibre rope as part of the rigging operation. Fastening a hook, making eyes for slings, and tying on a tagline are a few of these situations.

This section addresses the correct selection, inspection, and use of fibre rope for hoisting and rigging operations. It also explains how to tie several knots and hitches.

Characteristics

The fibres in these ropes are either natural or synthetic. Natural fibre ropes should be used cautiously for rigging since their strength is more variable than that of synthetic fibre ropes and they are much more subject to deterioration from rot, mildew, and chemicals.

Polypropylene is the most common fibre rope used in rigging. It floats but does not absorb water. It stretches less than other synthetic fibres such as nylon. It is affected, however, by the ultraviolet rays in sunlight and should not be left outside for long periods. It also softens with heat and is not recommended for work involving exposure to high heat.

Nylon fibre is remarkable for its strength. A nylon rope is considerably stronger than the same size and construction of polypropylene rope. But nylon stretches and hence is not used much for rigging. It is also more expensive, loses strength when wet, and has low resistance to acids.

Polyester ropes are stronger than polypropylene but not so strong as nylon. They have good resistance to acids, alkalis, and abrasion; do not stretch as much as nylon; resist degradation from ultraviolet rays; and don't soften in heat.

All fibre ropes conduct electricity when wet. When dry, however, polypropylene and polyester have much better insulating properties than nylon.

Inspection

Inspect fibre rope regularly and before each use. Any estimate of its capacity should be based on the portion of rope showing the most deterioration.

Check first for external wear and cuts, variations in the size and shape of strands, discolouration, and the elasticity or "life" remaining in the rope.

Untwist the strands without kinking or distorting them. The inside of the rope should be as bright and clean as when it was new. Check for broken yarns, excessively loose strands and yarns, or an accumulation of powdery dust, which indicates excessive internal wear between strands as the rope is flexed back and forth in use.

If the inside of the rope is dirty, if strands have started to unlay, or if the rope has lost life and elasticity, do not use it for hoisting.

Check for distortion in hardware. If thimbles are loose in the eyes, seize the eye to tighten the thimble (Figure 2.1). Ensure that all splices are in good condition and all tucks are done up (Figure 2.2).

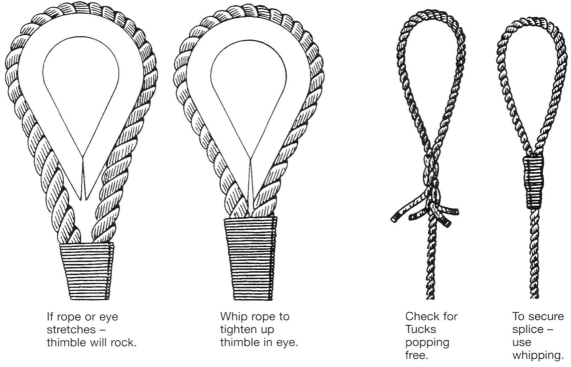

If rope or eye
stretches –
thimble will rock.

Whip rope to
tighten up
thimble in eye.

Check for
Tucks
popping
free.

To secure
splice –
use
whipping.

Figure 2.1   **Figure 2.2**

Minimum Breaking Strength and Working Load Limit

Minimum breaking strength (MBS) is the force at which a component may fail. The MBS is determined by the manufacturer, who also builds in a margin of safety called a **design factor (DF)**. Together, this allows them to assign a **working load limit (WLL)** to the component. For example, if a chain is manufactured with an MBS of 3,000 pounds and a DF of 3, the WLL of the chain will be 1/3 that of the MBS.

$$3,000 \text{ lb (MBS)} \div 3 \text{ (DF)} = 1,000 \text{ lb (WLL)}$$

Another margin of safety called a **safety factor (SF)** is often specified in health and safety legislation. It may be higher than the manufacturer's DF. If so, this would add an additional margin of safety to the component.

Let's apply a safety factor to the same chain used in the previous example. Section 172 (1)(d) of the Construction Projects regulation (O. Reg. 213/91) specifies that a hoisting and rigging device must "*be capable of supporting at least five times the maximum load to which it may be subjected*". Therefore, we apply an SF of 5.

Since this SF is higher than the manufacturer's DF, the WLL of the chain must be reduced from 1,000 pounds to 600 pounds in order to comply with the regulations.

$$(1,000 \text{ lb (mfg. WLL)} \times 3 \text{ (DF)}) \div 5 \text{ (SF)} = 600 \text{ lb (WLL)}$$

In addition, if you know the **working load (WL)** of an object to be hoisted and the appropriate SF, you can calculate the required capacity (i.e., MBS) of a component used to hoist that object. For example, a hoist rope used to lift a 250 pound load (WL) must have an SF of 5 (as per O. Reg. 213/91, s. 172 (1)(d)). This means that the rope must have an MBS of at least five times the weight of the load, which is 1,250 lb.

$$250 \text{ pounds (WL)} \times 5 \text{ (SF)} = 1,250 \text{ pounds (MBS)}$$

NOTE: When using fibre or wire hoist rope, take into consideratoin that the MBS refers to rope that is in good condition and is being used under normal working conditions. Many factors can weaken wire and fibre rope, thereby reducing its original ratedc apacity. These include:

- wear, age, overloading, broken fibres/wire
- shock loads
- minor inaccuracies in load weight calculations
- variances in strength caused by wetness, mildew, and degradation
- fibre yarns/wire strands weakened by ground-in dirt or other abrasive contaminants.

Select the appropriate rope based on the manufacturer's information, the conditions under which the rope will be used, and the degree of risk to life, limb, and property. It may be necessary to increase the SF to 10 or even 15 to account for these conditions.

> Similar to synthetic slings, you should only use clearly identified rope for hoisting. Identify all new rope by attaching a strong label showing the manufacturer's information.

Care

- To unwind a new coil of fibre rope, lay it flat with the inside end closest to the floor. Pull the inside end up through the coil and unwind counterclockwise.

- After use, recoil the rope clockwise. Keep looping the rope over your left arm until only about 15 feet remain. Start about a foot from the top of the coil and wrap the rope about six times around the loops. Then use your left hand to pull the bight back through the loops and tie with a couple of half-hitches to keep the loops from uncoiling (Figure 2.5).

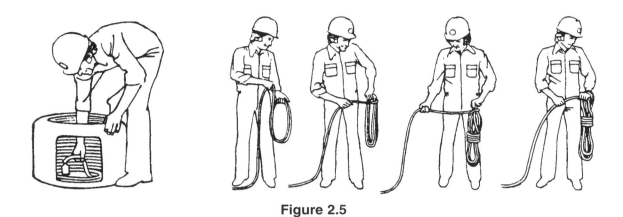

Figure 2.5

- Remove kinks carefully. Never try to pull them straight. This will severely damage the rope and reduce its strength.

- When a fibre rope is cut, the ends must be bound or whipped to keep the strands from untwisting. Figure 2.6 shows the right way to do this.

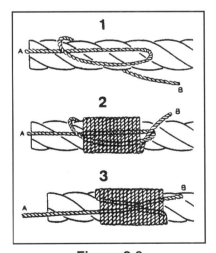

Figure 2.6

Storage

- Store fibre ropes in a dry cool room with good air circulation – temperature 10-21°C (50-70°F) humidity 40-60%.

- Hang fibre ropes in loose coils on large diameter wooden pegs well above the floor (Figure 2.7).

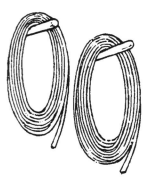

Figure 2.7

- Protect fibre ropes from weather, dampness, and sunlight. Keep them away from exhaust gases, chemical fumes, boilers, radiators, steam pipes, and other heat sources.
- Let fibre ropes dry before storing them. Moisture hastens rot and causes rope to kink easily. Let a frozen rope thaw completely before you handle it. Otherwise fibres can break. Let wet or frozen rope dry naturally.
- Wash dirty ropes in clean cool water and hang to dry.

Use

- Never overload a rope. Apply the design factor of 5 (10 for ropes used to support or hoist personnel). Then make further allowances for the rope's age and condition.
- Never drag a rope along the ground. Abrasive action will wear, cut, and fill the outside surfaces with grit.
- Never drag a rope over rough or sharp edges or across itself. Use softeners to protect rope at the sharp comers and edges of a load.
- Avoid all but straight line pulls with fibre rope. Bends interfere with stress distribution in fibres.
- Always use thimbles in rope eyes. Thimbles cut down on wear and stress.
- Keep sling angles at more than 45°. Lower angles can dramatically increase the load on each leg (Figure 2.8). The same is true with wire rope slings.

- Never use fibre rope near welding or flame cutting. Sparks and molten metal can cut through the rope or set it on fire.

- Keep fibre rope away from high heat. Don't leave it unnecessarily exposed to strong sunlight, which weakens and degrades the rope.

- Never couple left-lay rope to right-lay.

- When coupling wire and fibre ropes, always use metal thimbles in both eyes to keep the wire rope from cutting the fibre rope.

- Make sure that fibre rope used with tackle is the right size for the sheaves. Sheaves should have diameters at least six – preferably ten – times greater than the rope diameter.

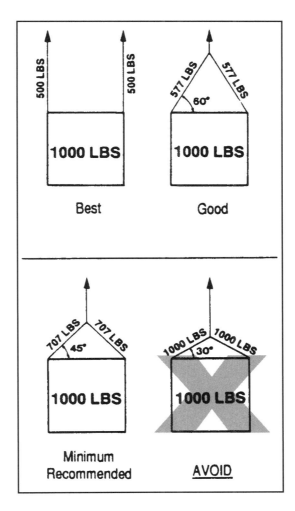

Figure 2.8

Knots

Wherever practical, avoid tying knots in rope. Knots, bends, and hitches reduce rope strength considerably. Just how much depends on the knot and how it is applied. Use a spliced end with a hook or other standard rigging hardware such as slings and shackles to attach ropes to loads.

In some cases, however, knots are more practical and efficient than other rigging methods, as for lifting and lowering tools or light material.

For knot tying, a rope is considered to have three parts (Figure 2.9).

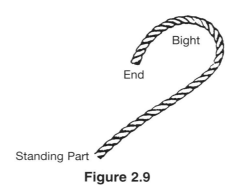

Figure 2.9

The **end** is where you tie the knot. The **standing part** is inactive. The **bight** is in between.

Following the right sequence is essential in tying knots. Equally important is the direction the end is to take and whether it goes over, under, or around other parts of the rope.

There are overhand loops, underhand loops, and turns (Figure 2.10).

Overhand Loop   Underhand Loop   Turn

Figure 2.10

WARNING – When tying knots, always follow the directions *over* and *under* precisely. If one part of the rope must go under another, do it that way. Otherwise an entirely different knot – or no knot at all – will result.

Once knots are tied, they should be drawn up slowly and carefully to make sure that sections tighten evenly and stay in proper position.

Bowline

Never jams or slips when properly tied. A universal knot if properly tied and untied. Two interlocking bowlines can be used to join two ropes together. Single bowlines can be used for hoisting or hitching directly around a ring.

Bowline on the Bight

Used to tie a bowline in the middle of a line or to make a set of double-leg spreaders for lifting pipe.

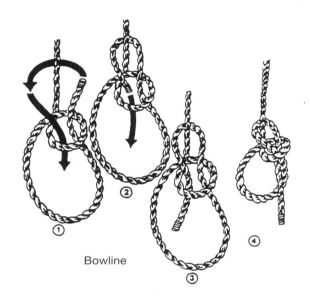

Bowline

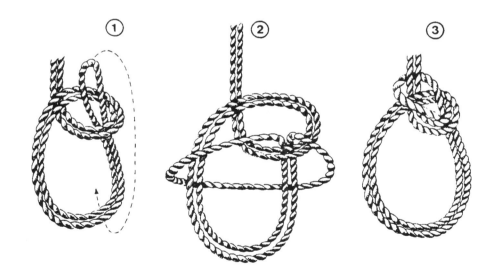

Pipe Hitch

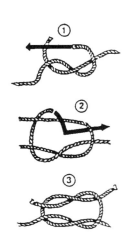

Reef or Square Knot

Can be used for tying two ropes of the same diameter together. It is unsuitable for wet or slippery ropes and should be used with caution since it unties easily when either free end is jerked. Both live and dead ends of the rope must come out of the loops at the same side.

Two Half Hitches

Two half hitches, which can be quickly tied, are reliable and can be put to almost any general use.

Two Half Hitches

Running Bowline

The running bowline is mainly used for hanging objects with ropes of different diameters. The weight of the object determines the tension necessary for the knot to grip.

Make an overhand loop with the end of the rope held toward you (1). Hold the loop with your thumb and fingers and bring the standing part of the rope back so that it lies behind the loop (2). Take the end of the rope in behind the standing part, bring it up, and feed it through the loop (3). Pass it behind the standing part at the top of the loop and bring it back down through the loop (4).

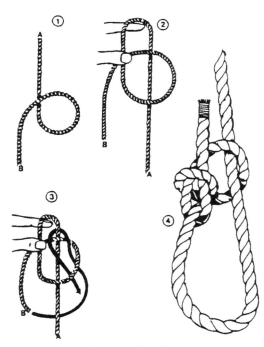

Running Bowline

Figure-Eight Knot

This knot is generally tied at the end of a rope to temporarily prevent the strands from unlaying. The figure-eight knot can be tied simply and quickly and will not jam as easily as the overhand knot. It is also larger, stronger, and does not injure the rope fibres. The figure-eight knot is useful in preventing the end of a rope from slipping through a block or an eye.

To tie the figure-eight knot, make an underhand loop (1). Bring the end around and over the standing part (2). Pass the end under and then through the loop (3). Draw up tight (4).

Figure Eight Knot

Hardware, Wire Rope, Slings

- **Wire Rope**
- **Sling Configurations**
- **Sling Angles**
- **Centre of Gravity**
- **Sling WLLs**
- **Sling Types**
- **Rigging Hardware**
- **Hoisting Tips**

Section 3

Hardware, Wire Rope, Slings

The rigger must be able to rig the load to ensure its stability when lifted. This requires a knowledge of safe sling configurations and the use of related hardware such as shackles, eyebolts, and wire rope clips.

Determining the working load limits of the rigging equipment as well as the weight of the load is a fundamental requirement of safe rigging practice.

Do not use any equipment that is suspected to be unsafe or unsuitable until its suitability has been verified by a competent person.

The working load limits of all hoisting equipment and rigging hardware are based on almost ideal conditions seldom achieved in the field. It is therefore important to recognize the factors such as wear, improper sling angles, point loading, and centre of gravity that can affect the rated working load limits of equipment and hardware.

This section describes the selection and safe use of various types of slings and different kinds of rigging hardware. Subjects include factors that can reduce capacity, inspection for signs of wear, calculating safe sling angles, and requirements for slings and hardware under the *Regulations for Construction Projects.*

Wire Rope

Selection

Proper rope selection will protect workers, the public, and property from harm and will get the job done well. An experienced rigger will be familiar with hoisting hazards and will have the best knowledge base for selecting the most appropriate rope for a specific lift. Some of the main aspects to consider are strength, diameter, grade, and the type of construction.

Wire Rope for Crane Hoists

The following are requirements when selecting wire rope for crane hoists:

1. The main hoisting rope must possess enough strength to take the maximum load that may be applied.

2. Wire ropes that are supplied as rigging on cranes must have the following design factors:

   - live or running ropes that wind on drums or pass over sheaves
     - 3.5 to 1
     - 5.0 to 1 when on a tower crane
   - pendants or standing ropes
     - 3.0 to 1

3. All wire rope must be
   - steel wire rope of the type, size, grade, and construction recommended by the manufacturer of the crane

- compatible with the sheaves and drum of the crane
- lubricated to prevent corrosion and wear.

4. The rope must *not* be spliced.

5. The rope must have its end connections securely fastened and kept with at least three full turns on the drum.

6. Rotation-resistant wire rope must *not* be used as cable for boom hoist reeving and pendants, or where an inner wire or strand is damaged or broken.

A properly selected rope will

- withstand repeated bending without failure of the wire strands from fatigue
- resist abrasion
- withstand distortion and crushing
- resist rotation
- resist corrosion.

Types of Construction

The number of wires in a rope is an important factor in determining a rope's characteristics. But the arrangement of the wires in the strand is also important.

Basic Types

The four basic constructions are illustrated in Figure 1 :

1. **Ordinary** – all wires are the same size.

2. **Warrington** – outer wires are alternately larger and smaller.

3. **Filler** – small wires fill spaces between larger wires.

4. **Seale** – wires of outer layer are larger diameter than wires of inner layer.

On ropes of **Ordinary** construction the strands are built in layers. The basic seven-wire strand consists of six wires laid around a central wire. A nineteen-wire strand is constructed by adding a layer of twelve wires over a seven-wire strand. Adding a third layer of eighteen wires results in a 37-wire strand.

In this type of construction the wires in each layer have different lay lengths. This means that the wires in adjacent layers contact each other at an angle. When the rope is loaded the wires rub against each other with a sawing action. This causes eventual failure of the wires at these points.

Ordinary Construction

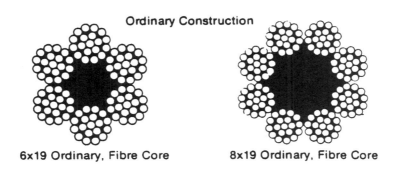

6x19 Ordinary, Fibre Core   8x19 Ordinary, Fibre Core

Warrington Construction

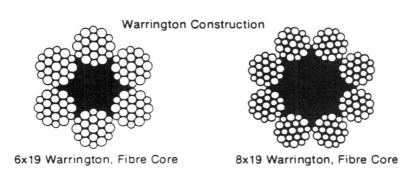

6x19 Warrington, Fibre Core   8x19 Warrington, Fibre Core

Seale Construction

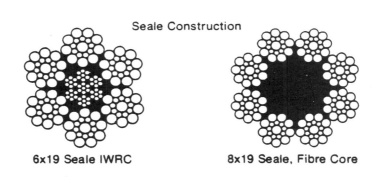

6x19 Seale IWRC   8x19 Seale, Fibre Core

Filler Construction

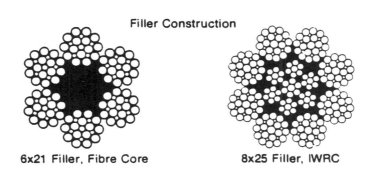

6x21 Filler, Fibre Core   8x25 Filler, IWRC

BASIC WIRE ROPE CONSTRUCTIONS
Figure 1

Wire Rope Inspection

It is essential to have a well-planned program of regular inspection carried out by an experienced inspector.

All wire rope in continuous service should be checked daily during normal operation and inspected on a weekly basis. A complete and thorough inspection of all ropes in use must be made at least once a month. Rope idle for a month or more should be given a thorough inspection before it is returned to service.

A record of each rope should include date of installation, size, construction, length, extent of service and any defects found.

The inspector will decide whether the rope must be removed from service. His decision will be based on:

1. details of the equipment on which the rope has been used,

2. maintenance history of the equipment,

3. consequences of failure, and

4. experience with similar equipment.

Conditions such as the following should be looked for during inspection.

Broken Wires

Occasional wire breaks are normal for most ropes and are not critical provided they are at well spaced intervals. Note the area and watch carefully for any further wire breaks. Broken wire ends should be removed as soon as possible by bending the broken ends back and forth with a pair of pliers. This way broken ends will be left tucked between the strands.

Construction regulations under The *Occupational Health and Safety Act* establish criteria for retiring a rope based on the number of wire breaks.

Worn and Abraded Wires

Abrasive wear causes the outer wires to become "D" shaped. These worn areas are often shiny in appearance (Figure 2). The rope must be replaced if wear exceeds 1/3 of the diameter of the wires.

Reduction in Rope Diameter

Reduction in rope diameter can be caused by abrasion of outside wires, crushing of the core, inner wire failure, or a loosening of the rope lay. All new ropes stretch slightly and decrease in diameter after being used.

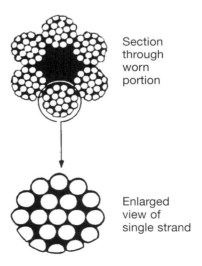

Section through worn portion

Enlarged view of single strand

When the surface wires are worn by 1/3 or more of their diameter, the rope must be replaced.

Figure 2

Snagged wires resulting from drum crushing

Rope that has been jammed after jumping off sheave

Rope subjected to drum crushing. Note the distortion of the individual wires and displacement from their original postion. This is usually caused by the rope scrubbing on itself.

Localized crushing of rope

Drum crushing

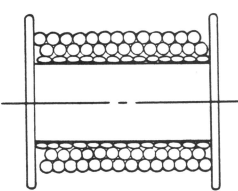

With no more than 2 layers on drum, use any kind of rope.

With more than 2 layers on drum, there is danger of crushing. Use larger rope or IWRC rope.

CRUSHED, JAMMED AND FLATTENED STRANDS
Figure 3

Rope Stretch

All steel ropes will stretch during initial periods of use. Called "constructional stretch", this condition is permanent. It results when wires in the strands and strands in the rope seat themselves under load. Rope stretch can be recognized by increased lay length. Six-strand ropes will stretch about six inches per 100 feet of rope while eight-strand ropes stretch approximately 10 inches per 100 feet. Rope stretched by more than this amount must be replaced.

Corrosion

Corrosion is a very dangerous condition because it can develop inside the rope without being seen. Internal rusting will accelerate wear due to increased abrasion as wires rub against one another. When pitting is observed, consider replacing the rope. Noticeable rusting and broken wires near attachments are also causes for replacement. Corrosion can be minimized by keeping the rope well lubricated.

Crushed, Flattened or Jammed Strands

These dangerous conditions require that the rope be replaced (Figure 3). They are often the result of crushing on the drum.

High Stranding and Unlaying

These conditions will cause the other strands to become overloaded. Replace the rope or renew the end connection to reset the rope lay (Figure 4).

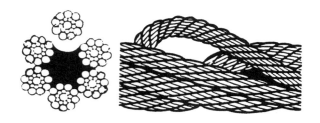

HIGH STRANDING
Figure 4

Bird Caging

Bird caging is caused by the rope being twisted or by a sudden release of an overload (Figure 5). The rope, or the affected section, must be replaced.

Multi-strand rope "birdcages" because of torsional unbalance.
Typical of buildup seen at anchorage end of multi-fall crane application.

A birdcage caused by sudden release of tension
and resulting rebound of rope from overloaded condition.
These strands and wires will **not** return to their original positions.

A birdcage which has been forced through a tight sheave.

BIRD CAGING
Figure 5

Kinks

Kinking is caused by loops that have been drawn too tightly as a result of improper handling (Figure 6). Kinks are permanent and will require that the rope, or damaged section, be taken out of service.

Core Protrusion

Core protrusion can be caused by shock loads and/or torsional imbalance (Figure 7). This condition requires that the rope be taken out of service.

Electrical Contact

Rope subjected to electrical contact will have wires that are fused, discoloured or annealed and must be removed from service.

An open kink like this is often caused by improper handling and uncoiling as shown.

These ropes show the severe damage resulting from the use of kinked ropes. Local wear, distortion, misplaced wires, and early failure are inevitable.

ROPE KINKS
Figure 6

Core protrusion as a result of torsional unbalance created by shock loading

Protrusion of IWRC from shock loading

CORE PROTRUSION
Figure 7

Figure 8 illustrates examples of rope damage, while Table 6 identifies likely causes of typical faults.

Narrow path of wear resulting in fatigue fractures caused by working in a grossly oversized groove or over small support rollers.

Breakup of IWRC from high stress. Note nicking of wires in outer strands

Two parallel paths of broken wires indicate bending through an undersize groove in the sheath.

Wire fractures at the strand or core interface, as distinct from crown fractures, caused by failure of core support.

Fatigue failure of wire rope subjected to heavy loads over small sheaves. In addition to the usual crown breaks, there are breaks in the valleys of the strands caused by strand nicking from overloading.

Wire rope shows severe wear and fatigue from running over small sheaves with heavy loads and constant abrasion.

Rope failing from fatigue after bending over small sheaves.

Wire rope that has jumped a sheave. The rope is deformed into a curl as though bent around a round shaft.

Mechanical damage due to rope movement over sharp edge under load.

Rope break due to excessive strain.

TYPICAL ROPE DAMAGE (continued on the next page)
Figure 8

Rapid appearance of many broken wires.

Wear and damage on one side of rope.

A single strand removed from a wire rope subjected to "strand nicking". This condition is the result of adjacent strands rubbing against one another and is usually caused by core failure due to continued operation of a rope under high tensile load. The ultimate result will be individual wire breaks in the valleys of the strands.

TYPICAL ROPE DAMAGE
Figure 8 (continued)

TABLE 6

FAULT	POSSIBLE CAUSE	FAULT	POSSIBLE CAUSE
Accelerated Wear	Severe abrasion from being dragged over the ground or obstructions. Rope wires too small for application or wrong construction or grade. Poorly aligned sheaves. Large fleet angle. Worm sheaves with improper groove size or shape. Sheaves, rollers and fairleads having rough wear surfaces. Stiff or seized sheave bearings. High bearing and contact pressures.	Broken Wires or Undue Wear on One Side of Rope	Improper alignment. Damaged sheaves and drums.
		Broken Wires Near Fittings	Rope vibration.
		Burns	Sheave groove too small. Sheaves too heavy. Sheave bearings seized. Rope dragged over obstacle.
Rapid Appearance of Broken Wires	Rope is not flexible enough. Sheaves, rollers, drums too small in diameter. Overload and shock load. Excessive rope vibration. Rope speed too high. Kinks that have formed and been straightened out. Crushing and flattening of the rope. Reverse bends. Sheave wobble.	Rope Core Charred	Excessive heat.
		Corrugation and Excessive Wear	Rollers too soft. Sheave and drum material too soft.
		Distortion of Lay	Rope improperly cut. Core failure. Sheave grooves too big.
		Pinching and Crushing	Sheave grooves too small.
Rope Broken Off Square	Overload, shock load. Kink. Broken or cracked sheave flange.	Rope Chatters	Rollers too small.
Strand Break	Overload, shock load. Local wear. Slack in 1 or more strands.	Rope Unlays	Swivel fittings on Lang Lay ropes. Rope dragging against stationary object.
		Crushing and Nicking	Rope struck or hit during handling.
Corrosion	Inadequate lubricant. Improper type of lubricant. Improper storage. Exposure to acids or alkalis.	High Stranding	Fittings improperly attached. Broken strand. Kinks, dog legs. Improper seizing.
Kinks, Dog Legs, Distortions	Improper installation. Improper handling.	Reduction in Diameter	Broken core. Overload. Corrosion. Severe wear.
Excessive Wear in Spots	Kinks or bends in rope due to improper handling in service or during installation. Vibration of rope on drums or sheaves.	Bird Cage	Sudden release of load.
Crushing and Flattening	Overload, shock load. Uneven spooling. Cross winding. Too much rope on drum. Loose bearing on drum. Faulty clutches. Rope dragged over obstacle.	Strand Nicking	Core failure due to continued operation under high load.
Stretch	Overload. Untwist of Lang Lay ropes.	Core Protrusion	Shock loading. Disturbed rope lay. Rope unlays. Load spins.

Procedures and Precautions with Wire Rope

- Ensure that the right size and construction of rope is used for the job.

- Inspect and lubricate rope regularly according to manufacturer's guidelines.

- Never overload the rope. Minimize shock loading. To ensure there is no slack in the rope, start the load carefully, applying power smoothly and steadily.

- Take special precautions and/or use a larger size rope whenever

  - the exact weight of the load is unknown

  - there is a possibility of shock loading

  - conditions are abnormal or severe

  - there are hazards to personnel.

- Use softeners to protect rope from corners and sharp edges.

- Avoid dragging rope out from under loads or over obstacles.

- Do not drop rope from heights.

- Store all unused rope in a clean, dry place.

- Never use wire rope that has been cut, kinked, or crushed.

- Ensure that rope ends are properly seized.

- Use thimbles in eye fittings at all times.

- Prevent loops in slack lines from being pulled tight and kinking. If a loop forms, don't pull it out — unfold it. Once a wire rope is kinked, damage is permanent. A weak spot will remain no matter how well the kink is straightened out.

- Check for abnormal line whip and vibration.

- Avoid reverse bends.

- Ensure that drums and sheaves are the right diameter for the rope being used.

- Ensure that sheaves are aligned and that fleet angle is correct.

- Sheaves with deeply worn or scored grooves, cracked or broken rims, and worn or damaged bearings must be replaced.

- Ensure that rope spools properly on the drum. Never wind more than the correct amount of rope on any drum. Never let the rope cross-wind.

Slings

General

Slings are often severely worn and abused in construction. Damage is caused by:

- failure to provide blocking or softeners between slings and load, thereby allowing sharp edges or comers of the load to cut or abrade the slings
- pulling slings out from under loads, leading to abrasion and kinking
- shock loading that increases the stress on slings that may already be overloaded
- traffic running over slings, especially tracked equipment.

Because of these and other conditions, as well as errors in calculating loads and estimating sling angles, it is strongly recommended that working load limits be based on a design factor of at least 5:1.

For the same reasons, slings must be carefully inspected before each use.

Sling Angles

The rated capacity of any sling depends on its size, its configuration, and the angles formed by its legs with the horizontal.

For instance, a two-leg sling used to lift 1000 pounds will have a 500-pound load on each leg at a sling angle of 90°. The load on each leg will go up as the angle goes down. At 30° the load will be 1000 pounds on each leg! See Figure 9.

Keep sling angles greater than 45° whenever possible. The use of any sling at an angle lower than 30° is extremely hazardous. This is especially true when an error of only 5° in estimating the sling angle can be so dangerous.

Sling Configurations

Slings are not only made of various material such as wire rope and nylon web. They also come in various configurations for different purposes. Common configurations are explained on the following pages.

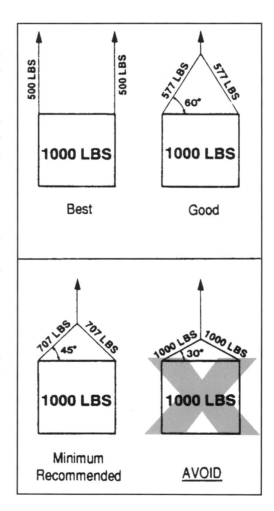

Figure 9

Sling Configurations

The term "sling" covers a wide variety of configurations for fibre ropes, wire ropes, chains and webs. Correct application of slings commonly used in construction will be explained here because improper application can be dangerous.

The **Single Vertical Hitch** (Figure 10) supports a load by a single vertical part or leg of the sling. The total weight of the load is carried by a single leg, the sling angle is 90° (sling angle is measured from the horizontal) and the weight of the load can equal the working load limit of the sling and fittings. End fittings can vary but thimbles should be used in the eyes. The eye splices on wire ropes should be Mechanical-Flemish Splices for best security.

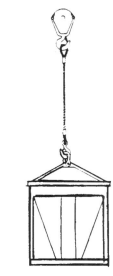

SINGLE VERTICAL HITCH
Figure 10

The single vertical hitch must not be used for lifting loose material, lengthy material or anything difficult to balance. This hitch provides absolutely no control over the load because it permits rotation. Use single vertical hitches on items equipped with lifting eyebolts or shackles.

Bridle Hitch (Figs 11, 13.). Two, three or four single hitches can be used together to form a bridle hitch for hoisting an object with the necessary lifting lugs or attachments. Used with a wide assortment of end fittings, bridle hitches provide excellent load stability when the load is distributed equally among the legs, the hook is directly over the load's centre of gravity and the load is raised level. To distribute the load equally it may be necessary to adjust the leg lengths with turnbuckles. Proper use of a bridle hitch requires that sling angles be carefully measured to ensure that individual legs are not overloaded.

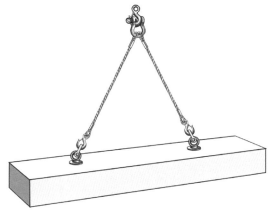

Figure 11

Because the load may not be distributed evenly when a four-leg sling lifts a rigid load, assume that the load is carried by two of the legs only and "rate" the four-leg sling as a two-leg sling.

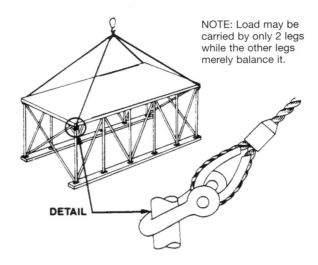

NOTE: Load may be carried by only 2 legs while the other legs merely balance it.

DETAIL

4-LEG BRIDLE HITCH
Figure 13

The **Single Basket Hitch** (Figure 14) is used to support a load by attaching one end of the sling to the hook, then passing the other end under the load and attaching it to the hook. Ensure that the load does not turn or slide along the rope during a lift.

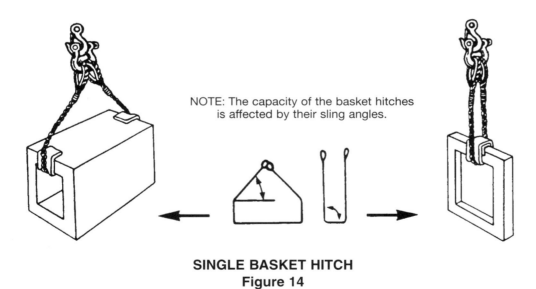

NOTE: The capacity of the basket hitches is affected by their sling angles.

SINGLE BASKET HITCH
Figure 14

The **Double Basket Hitch** (Figure 15) consists of two single basket hitches placed under the load. On smooth surfaces the legs will tend to draw together as the load is lifted. To counter this, brace the hitch against a change in contour, or other reliable means, to prevent the slings from slipping. You must keep the legs far enough apart to provide balance, but not so far apart that they create angles below 60 degrees from the horizontal. On smooth surfaces, a **Double Wrap Basket Hitch** may be a better choice.

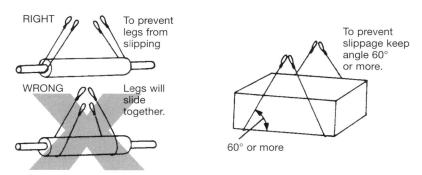

DOUBLE BASKET HITCHES
Figure 15

The **Double Wrap Basket Hitch** (Figure 16) is a basket hitch wrapped completely around the load and compressing it rather than merely supporting it, as does the ordinary basket hitch. The double wrap basket hitch can be used in pairs like the double basket hitch. This method is excellent for handling loose material, pipe, rod or smooth cylindrical loads because the sling is in full 360° contact with the load and tends to draw it together.

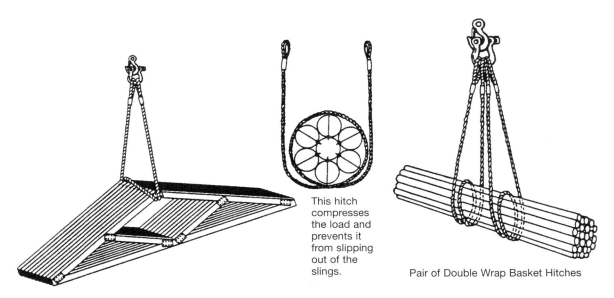

DOUBLE WRAP BASKET HITCH
Figure 16

The **Single Choker Hitch** (Figure 17) forms a noose in the rope. It does not provide full 360° contact with the load, however, and therefore should not be used to lift loads difficult to balance or loosely bundled. Choker hitches are useful for turning loads and for resisting a load that wants to turn.

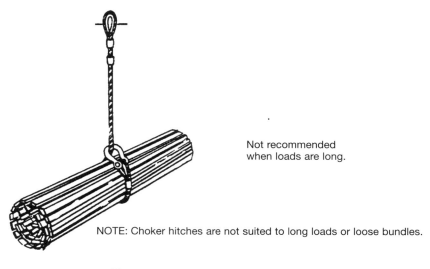

Not recommended
when loads are long.

NOTE: Choker hitches are not suited to long loads or loose bundles.

Chokers do not provide full support for loose loads – material can fall out.

SINGLE CHOKER HITCH
Figure 17

Using a choker hitch with two legs (Figure 18) provides stability for longer loads. Like the single choker, this configuration does not completely grip the load. You must lift the load horizontally with slings of even length to prevent the load from sliding out. You should lift loosely-bundled loads with a Double Wrap Choker Hitch.

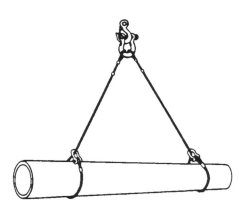

Figure 18

A **Double Wrap Choker Hitch** (Figure 19) is formed by wrapping the sling completely around the load and hooking it into the vertical part of the sling. This hitch is in full 360° contact with the load and tends to draw it tightly together. It can be used either singly on short, easily balanced loads or in pairs on longer loads.

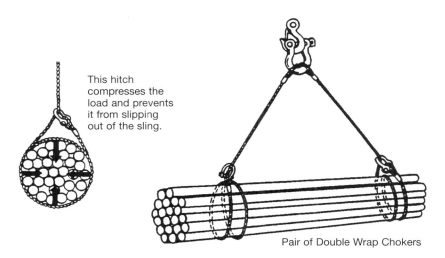

This hitch compresses the load and prevents it from slipping out of the sling.

Pair of Double Wrap Chokers

DOUBLE WRAP CHOKER HITCHES
Figure 19

Endless Slings or Grommet Slings (Figure 20) are useful for a variety of applications. Endless chain slings are manufactured by attaching the ends of a length of chain with a welded or mechanical link. Endless web slings are sewn. An endless wire rope sling is made from one continuous strand wrapped onto itself to form a six-strand rope with a strand core. The end is tucked into the body at the point where the strand was first laid onto itself. These slings can be used in a number of configurations, as vertical hitches, basket hitches, choker hitches and combinations of these basic arrangements. They are very flexible but tend to wear more rapidly than other slings because they are not normally equipped with fittings and thus are deformed when bent over hooks or choked.

NOTE: Ensure that the splice is always clear of the hooks and load.

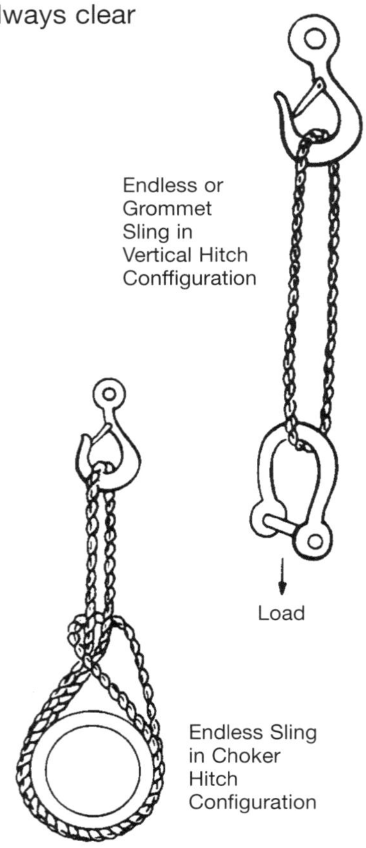

Endless or Grommet Sling in Vertical Hitch Conffiguration

Load

Endless Sling in Choker Hitch Configuration

ENDLESS OR GROMMET SLINGS
Figure 20

Braided Slings (Figure 21) are usually fabricated from six to eight small-diameter ropes braided together to form a single rope that provides a large bearing surface, tremendous strength, and flexibility in every direction. They are easy to handle and almost impossible to kink. The braided sling can be used in all the standard configurations and combinations but is especially useful for basket hitches where low bearing pressure is desirable or where the bend is extremely sharp.

BRAIDED SLINGS
Figure 21

Sling Angles

The total weight that you can pick up with a set of slings is reduced when the slings are used at angles (formed the with horizontal). For instance, two slings used to lift 1000 pounds will have a 500-pound force on each sling (or leg) at a sling angle of 90 degrees (see Figure 22b). The force on each leg increases as the angle goes down. At 30 degrees the force will be 1000 pounds on each leg!

Keep sling angles greater than 45 degrees whenever possible. Using any sling at an angle lower than 30 degrees is extremely hazardous. In such cases, an error of 5 degrees in estimating the sling can be very dangerous. The sharp increase in loading at low angles is clearly shown in Figure 22a.

Low sling angles also create large, compressive forces on the load that may cause buckling—especially in longer flexible loads.

EFFECT OF SLING ANGLE ON SLING LOAD

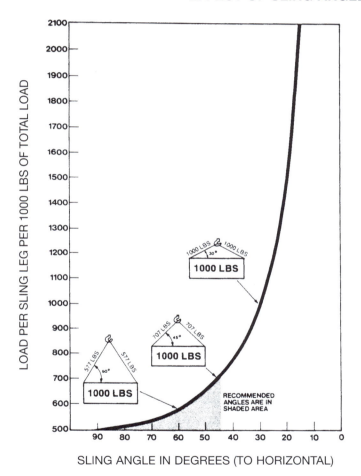

Figure 22a

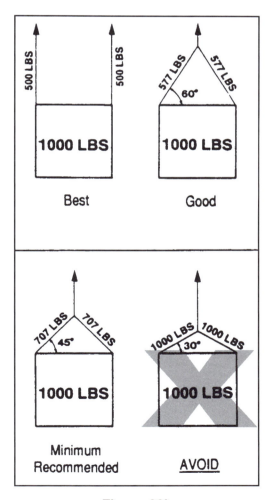

Figure 22b

49

Some load tables list sling angles as low as 15° but the use of any sling at an angle less than 30° is extremely dangerous. Not only are the loads in each leg high at these low angles but an error in measurement as little as 5° can affect the load in the sling drastically. For example, the data in Figure 23 illustrates the effect of a 5° error in angle measurement on the sling load. Notice that there is a 50% error in the assumed load at the 15° sling angle.

Figure 23

EXAMPLE OF THE EFFECT OF SLING ANGLE MEASUREMENT ERROR ON LOADS				
Assumed Sling Angle	Assumed Load (Pounds Per Leg)	Actual Angle (is 5° Less Than Assumed Angle)	Actual Load (Pounds Per Leg)	Error %
90°	500	85°	502	0.4
75°	518	70°	532	2.8
60°	577	55°	610	5.7
45°	707	40°	778	9.1
30°	1,000	25°	1,183	18.3
15°	1,932	10°	2,880	49.0

Centre of Gravity

It is always important to rig the load so that it is stable. The load's centre of gravity must be directly under the main hook and below the lowest sling attachment point before the load is lifted (Figure 24).

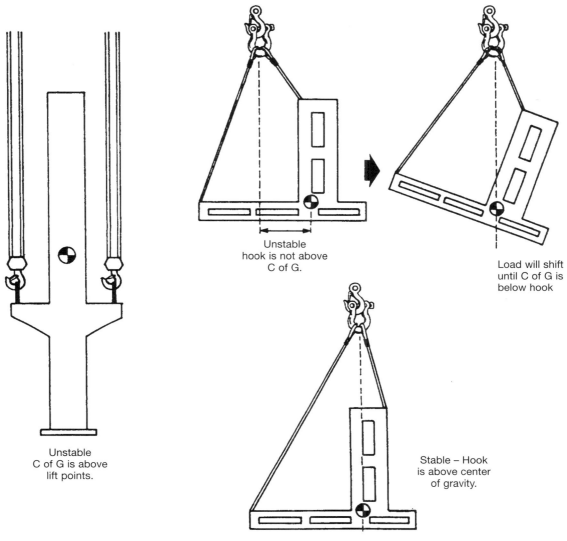

Unstable
C of G is above
lift points.

Unstable
hook is not above
C of G.

Load will shift
until C of G is
below hook

Stable – Hook
is above center
of gravity.

EFFECT OF CENTRE OF GRAVITY ON LIFT
Figure 24

Centre of gravity is the point around which an object's weight is evenly balanced. The entire weight may be considered concentrated at this point. A suspended object will always move until its centre of gravity is directly below its suspension point. To make a level or stable lift, the crane or hook block must be directly above this point **before the load is lifted**. Thus a load which is slung above and through the centre of gravity will not topple or slide out of the slings (Figure 25).

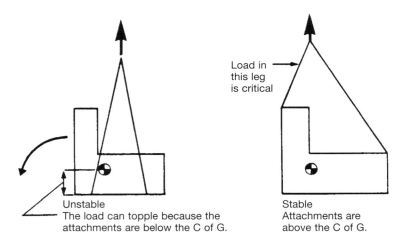

Load in
this leg
is critical

Unstable
The load can topple because the
attachments are below the C of G.

Stable
Attachments are
above the C of G.

EFFECT OF CENTRE OF GRAVITY ON LIFT
Figure 25

If an object is symmetrical in shape and uniform in composition, its centre of gravity will lie at its geometric centre. The centre of gravity of an oddly shaped object, however, can be difficult to locate. One way to estimate its location is to guess where the centre of gravity lies, rig the load accordingly, signal for a trial lift, and then watch the movement of the suspended load. The centre of gravity will seek to move, within the constraints of your rigging, toward the line drawn vertically from the hook to the ground (just like a plumb bob). Adjust the sling suspension for the best balance and stability.

The centre of gravity always seeks out the lowest point toward the ground. For this reason, the sling attachment points on your load should be located above the centre of gravity whenever practical. If the sling attachment points lie below the centre of gravity, your load could flip over or topple.

When the centre of gravity is closer to one sling leg than to the other, the closest sling leg bears a greater share of the weight.

When a load tilts after it is lifted, the tension increases in one sling leg and decreases on the other sling leg. If your load tilts, land the load and rig it again to equalize the load on each leg.

Working Load Limits

Knowledge of working load limits (WLLs) is essential to the use of ropes, slings, and rigging hardware. As indicated in previous sections, the working load limit should be stamped, pressed, printed, tagged, or otherwise indicated on all rigging equipment.

Field Calculation Formula

The **field calculation formula** can be used to compute the working load limit of a wire rope in tons (2,000 pounds). The formula applies to new wire rope of Improved Plow steel and a design factor of 5.

$$WLL = DIAMETER \times DIAMETER \times 8$$
(where DIAMETER = nominal rope diameter in inches)
OR
$$WLL = D^2 \times 8$$

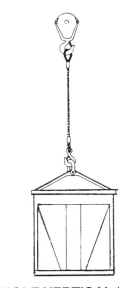

SINGLE VERTICAL HITCH

Examples:

(a) 1/2 inch diameter rope

WLL = 1/2 x 1/2 x 8 = 2 tons

(b) 5/8 inch diameter rope

WLL = 5/8 x - 5/8 x 8 = 3.125 tons

(c) 1 inch diameter rope

WLL = 1 x 1 x 8 = 8 tons

Sling Angle and WLL

In rigging tables, sling capacities are related to set angles of 90 degrees, 60 degrees, 45 degrees, and 30 degrees. Measuring angles in the field can be difficult; however, you can determine three of them with readily available tools. When a 90-degree angle is formed at the crane hook, you can measure this with a square. It forms two 45-degree angles at the load (see Figure 26).

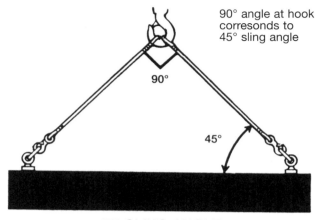

45° SLING ANGLE
Figure 26

A 60-degree angle can also be easily identified (see Figure 27). With a two-leg bridal hitch, a 60-degree angle is formed when the distance between the attachment points on the load equals the length of the sling leg.

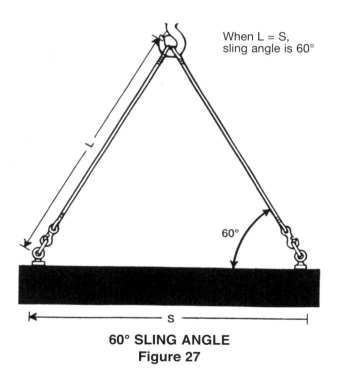

60° SLING ANGLE
Figure 27

Estimating Sling WLLs

Because it is difficult to remember all load, size, and sling angle combinations provided in tables, some general rules can be used to estimate working load limits for common sling configurations.

Each rule is based on the working load limit of a single vertical hitch of a given size and material and on the ratio **H/L**.

H is the vertical distance from the saddle of the hook to the top of the load. **L** is the distance, measured along the sling, from the saddle of the hook to the top of the load (Figure 28).

If you cannot measure the entire length of the sling, measure along the sling from the top of the load to a convenient point and call this distance **l**. From this point measure down to the load and call this distance **h**. The ratio **h/l** will be the same as the ratio **H/L** (Figure 28).

The ratio of height (H) to length of the sling (L) provides the reduction in capacity due to the sling angle. This gives you the value of the reduced capacity of a single vertical hitch. If there are more than two slings and *the load is shared equally by all legs,* you can increase this reduced capacity. The capacity is increased (multiplied) by the number of legs (see 3- and 4-leg hitches on the next page).

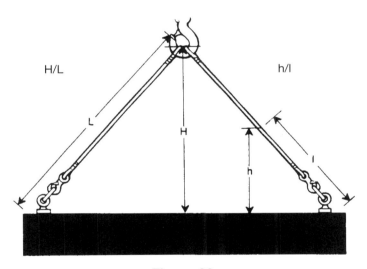

Figure 28

H/L or **h/l** will apply equally to the following rules for different sling configurations. The efficiencies of end fittings must also be considered to determine the capacity of the sling assembly.

REMEMBER: the smaller the sling angle, the lower the working load limit.

Bridle Hitches (2-Leg) (Figure 29)

The formula for the WLL of a two-leg bridal hitch is:

WLL (of two-leg hitch) = WLL (of single vertical hitch) x H/L x 2

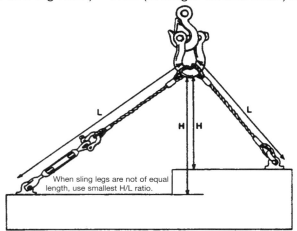

When sling legs are not of equal length, use smallest H/L ratio.

DETERMINING CAPACITY OF 2-LEG BRIDLE HITCHES
Figure 29

Bridle Hitches (3- and 4-Leg) (Figures 30 and 31)

The formula for the WLL of a 3-leg bridal hitch is:

WLL (3-leg hitch) = WLL (single vertical hitch) x H/L x 3

The formula for the WLL of a 4-leg bridal hitch is:

WLL (4-leg hitch) = WLL (single vertical hitch) x H/L x 4

Three-leg hitches are less susceptible to unequal distribution since the load can tilt and equalize the loads in each leg. However, lifting an irregularly shaped, rigid load with a three-leg hitch may develop unequal loads in the sling legs. To be safe, use the formula for a two-leg bridle hitch under such circumstances.

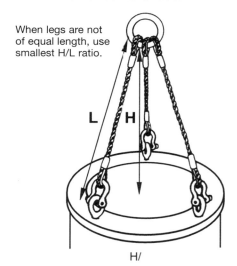

When legs are not of equal length, use smallest H/L ratio.

DETERMINING CAPACITY OF 3-LEG BRIDLE HITCH
Figure 30

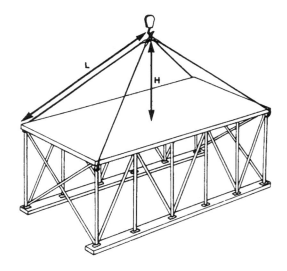

DETERMINING CAPACITY OF 4-LEG BRIDLE HITCH
Figure 31

Note: With 3- and 4-leg bridal hitches, the load can be carried by only two legs while the third and fourth legs simply balance the load. Therefore, in these situations you should be cautious and use the formula for a 2-leg configuration.

Remember that the rated capacity of a multi-leg sling is based on the assumption that all legs are used. If this is not the case, de-rate the sling assembly accordingly and hook all unused legs to the crane hook so they will not become snagged during the lift.

Single Basket Hitch (Figure 32)

For vertical legs – WLL = WLL (of Single Vertical Hitch) x 2
For inclined legs – WLL = WLL (of Single Vertical Hitch) x H/L x 2

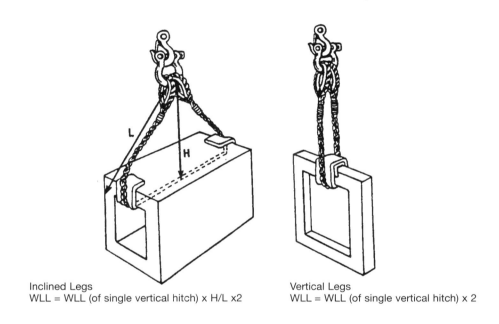

Inclined Legs
WLL = WLL (of single vertical hitch) x H/L x2

Vertical Legs
WLL = WLL (of single vertical hitch) x 2

DETERMINING CAPACITY OF SINGLE BASKET HITCH
Figure 32

Double Basket Hitch

For vertical legs:
WLL = WLL (of single vertical hitch) x 3

For inclined legs:
WLL = WLL (of single vertical hitch) x H/L x 3

Double Wrap Basket Hitch
Depending on configuration, WLLs are the same as for the single basket or double basket hitch.

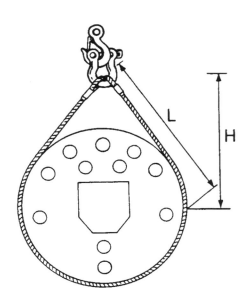

DETERMINING CAPACITY OF DOUBLE BASKET HITCH WITH INCLINED LEGS

Single Choker Hitch
For choker angles of 45 degrees or more:
WLL = WLL (of single vertical hitch) x 3/4

A choker angle less than 45 degrees (formed by the choker) is not recommended due to extreme loading on the sling. If the angle *does* go below 45 degrees, use caution because it could slip tighter during the lift. Apply the following formula:

WLL = WLL (of single vertical hitch) x A/B

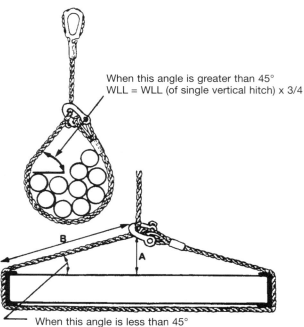

When this angle is greater than 45°
WLL = WLL (of single vertical hitch) x 3/4

When this angle is less than 45°
WLL = WLL (of single vertical hitch) x A/B

DETERMINING CAPACITY OF SINGLE CHOKER HITCH

Endless and Grommet Slings
Although grommet slings support a load with two legs, their working load limit is usually taken as 1.5 times the working load limit of a single vertical hitch. This reduction allows for capacity lost because of sharp bends at the hook or shackle.

Two-Leg Choker Hitches

With two-leg choker hitches there are two reductions to consider:

1. the angles formed by the choker
2. the angle formed by the sling (bridal hitch).

For bridal-hitch sling angles:
WLL = WLL (of single vertical hitch) x H/L x 2

For choker angles of 45 degrees or more:
WLL = WLL (of single vertical hitch) x 3/4

A choker angle less than 45 degrees (formed by the choker) is not recommended due to extreme loading of the sling. If the angle *does* go below 45 degrees, use caution because it can slip tighter during the lift. Apply the following formula: WLL = WLL (of single vertical hitch) x A/B

When you calculate both reductions together, the WLL is calculated as follows:
WLL = WLL (of single vertical hitch) x H/L x 2 x 3/4.

Or, for small choker angles, the formula is:
WLL = WLL (of single vertical hitch) x H/L x 2 x A/B.

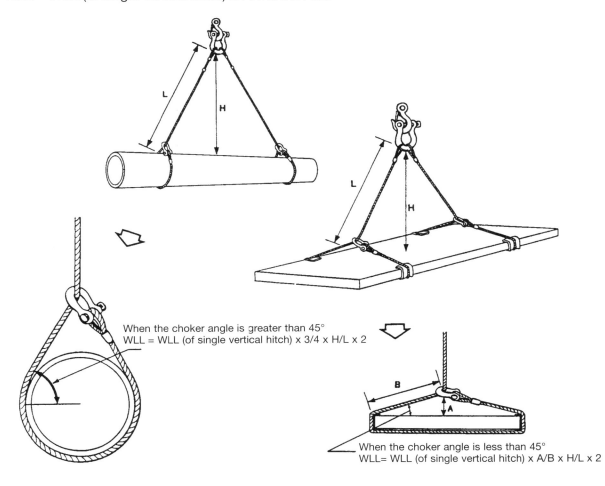

When the choker angle is greater than 45°
WLL = WLL (of single vertical hitch) x 3/4 x H/L x 2

When the choker angle is less than 45°
WLL= WLL (of single vertical hitch) x A/B x H/L x 2

DETERMINING CAPACITY OF DOUBLE CHOKER HITCH

Double Wrap Choker Hitch
Depending on configuration, working load limits are the same as for the Single Choker Hitch or the Double Choker Hitch.

59

Types of Slings

Wire rope slings should be inspected frequently for broken wires, kinks, abrasion and corrosion. Inspection procedures and replacement criteria outlined in the session on wire rope apply and must be followed regardless of sling type or application.

All wire rope slings should be made of improved plow steel with independent wire rope cores to reduce the risk of crushing. Manufacturers will assist in selecting the rope construction for a given application.

It is recommended that all eyes in wire rope slings be equipped with thimbles, be formed with the Flemish Splice and be secured by swaged or pressed mechanical sleeves or fittings. With the exception of socketed connections, this is the only method that produces an eye as strong as the rope itself, with reserve strength should the mechanical sleeve or fitting fail or loosen.

The capacity of a wire rope sling can be greatly affected by being bent sharply around pins, hooks or parts of a load. The wire rope industry uses the term "D/d ratio" to express the severity of bend. "D" is the diameter of curvature that the rope or sling is subjected to and "d" is the diameter of the rope.

Wire Rope Slings

The use of wire rope slings for lifting materials provides several advantages over other types of sling. While not as strong as chain, it has good flexibility with minimum weight. Breaking outer wires warn of failure and allow time to react. Properly fabricated wire rope slings are very safe for general construction use.

On smooth surfaces, the basket hitch should be snubbed against a step or change of contour to prevent the rope from slipping as load is applied. The angle between the load and the sling should be approximately 60 degrees or greater to avoid slippage.

On wooden boxes or crates, the rope will dig into the wood sufficiently to prevent slippage. On other rectangular loads, the rope should be protected by guards or load protectors at the edges to prevent kinking.

Loads should not be allowed to turn or slide along the rope during a lift. The sling or the load may become scuffed or damaged.

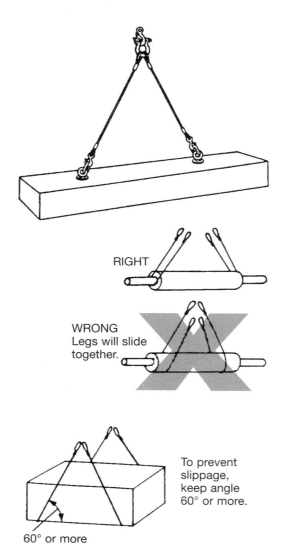

RIGHT

WRONG
Legs will slide together.

To prevent slippage, keep angle 60° or more.

60° or more

Working Load Limit (WLL): Tons of 2000 lbs
UNI-LOC® 6-strand Wire Rope Slings
- 6 x 19, 6 x 26, 6 x 25 and 6 x 36 IWRC -
Design Factor = 5

Nom. Rope Dia. Inch	Vertical	Choker	2 Sling Bridle, or single Basket Hitch			Weight of one 10 ft long Std Loop Sling w/o any hardware approx. lbs
			60°	45°	30°	
1/4	0.65	0.48	1.1	0.91	0.65	1.6
3/8	1.4	1.1	2.5	2.0	1.4	3.5
1/2	2.5	1.9	4.4	3.6	2.5	6.8
5/8	3.9	2.9	6.8	5.5	3.9	10.9
3/4	5.6	4.1	9.7	7.9	5.6	16.5
7/8	7.6	5.6	13	11	7.6	23.5
1	9.8	7.2	17	14	9.8	32.5
1-1/8	12	9.1	21	17	12	41.0
1-1/4	15	11	26	21	15	53.5
1-3/8	18	13	31	25	18	68.5
1-1/2	21	16	37	30	21	85.0
1-3/4	28	21	49	40	28	130.0
2	37	28	63	52	37	178.0
2-1/4	44	35	77	63	44	243.0
2-1/2	54	42	94	77	54	315.0

For Choker Bridle Sling, multiply values by 3/4.

For Double Basket Sling, multiply values by 2.

NOTES: 1) Working Load Limit (WLL) based on **UNI-LOC®** splice only.
2) Values for Chokers valid only if A is greater than 30˚.
3) Values based on ropes with a tensile strength of EIPS.
4) Shackles and fittings must be sized to the full WLL of sling.
5) WLL Basket Hitch is based on D/d ratio of 25.

Reprinted with permission from UNIROPE Ltd.

Chain Slings

Chain slings are suited to applications requiring flexibility and resistance to abrasion, cutting and high temperatures.

Alloy steel chain grade 80 is marked with an 8, 80, or 800; grade 100 is marked with a 10, 100, or 1000. Alloy steel chain is the only type which can be used for overhead lifting.

As with all slings and associated hardware, chain slings must have a design factor of 5. In North America, chain manufacturers usually give working load limits based on a design factor of 3.5 or 4. Always check with manufacturers to determine the design factor on which their working load limits are based.

If the design factor is less than 5, calculate the working load limit of the chain by multiplying the catalogue working load limit by the manufacturer's design factor and dividing by 5.

$$\frac{\text{CATALOGUE WLL x MANUFACTURER'S D.F.}}{5} = \text{WLL (based on design factor of 5)}$$

Example – 1/2" Alloy Steel Chain

Catalogue WLL = 13,000 lbs.
Design Factor = 3.5
$$\frac{13,000 \text{ lbs}}{5} \times 3.5 = 9,100 \text{ lbs.}$$

This chain sling must be de-rated to 9,100 lbs. for construction applications.

Wherever they bear on sharp edges, chain slings should be padded to prevent links from being bent and to protect the load. Never tie a knot in a chain sling to shorten the reach. Slings can be supplied with grab hooks or shortening clutches for such applications.

Inspect chain slings for inner link wear and wear on the outside of the link barrels (Figure 33). Manufacturers publish tables of allowable wear for various link sizes. Many companies will also supply wear gauges to indicate when a sling must be retired or links replaced. Gauges or tables from a particular manufacturer should only be used on that brand of chain since exact dimensions of a given nominal size can vary from one manufacturer to another.

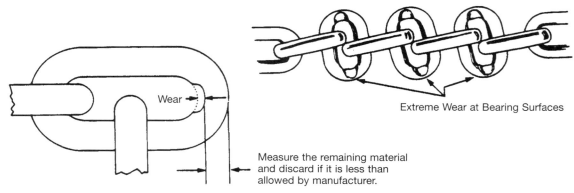

Wear

Measure the remaining material and discard if it is less than allowed by manufacturer.

Extreme Wear at Bearing Surfaces

INSPECT ALL LINKS FOR WEAR AT BEARING SURFACES
Figure 33

A competent worker should check chain slings for nicks and gouges that may cause stress concentrations and weaken links (Figure 34). If nicks or gouges are deep or large in area, or reduce link size below allowable wear, remove the chain from service. Any repairs must be done according to manufacturers' specifications.

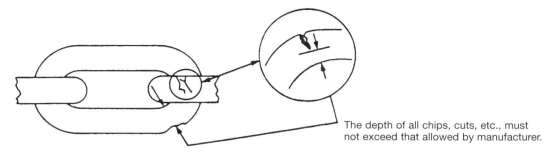

The depth of all chips, cuts, etc., must not exceed that allowed by manufacturer.

INSPECT ALL LINKS FOR GOUGES, CHIPS AND CUTS
Figure 34

Never use repair links or mechanical coupling links to splice broken lengths of alloy steel chain. They are much weaker than the chain links. Never use a chain if the links are stretched or do not move freely.

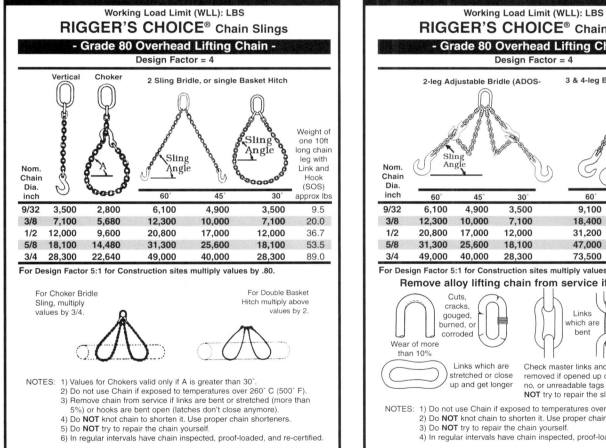

Working Load Limit (WLL): LBS
RIGGER'S CHOICE® Chain Slings
- Grade 80 Overhead Lifting Chain -
Design Factor = 4

Nom. Chain Dia. inch	Vertical	Choker	2 Sling Bridle, or single Basket Hitch			Weight of one 10ft long chain leg with Link and Hook (SOS) approx lbs
			60°	45°	30°	
9/32	3,500	2,800	6,100	4,900	3,500	9.5
3/8	7,100	5,680	12,300	10,000	7,100	20.0
1/2	12,000	9,600	20,800	17,000	12,000	36.7
5/8	18,100	14,480	31,300	25,600	18,100	53.5
3/4	28,300	22,640	49,000	40,000	28,300	89.0

For Design Factor 5:1 for Construction sites multiply values by .80.

For Choker Bridle Sling, multiply values by 3/4.

For Double Basket Hitch multiply above values by 2.

NOTES: 1) Values for Chokers valid only if A is greater than 30°.
2) Do not use Chain if exposed to temperatures over 260° C (500° F).
3) Remove chain from service if links are bent or stretched (more than 5%) or hooks are bent open (latches don't close anymore).
4) Do **NOT** knot chain to shorten it. Use proper chain shorteners.
5) Do **NOT** try to repair the chain yourself.
6) In regular intervals have chain inspected, proof-loaded, and re-certified.

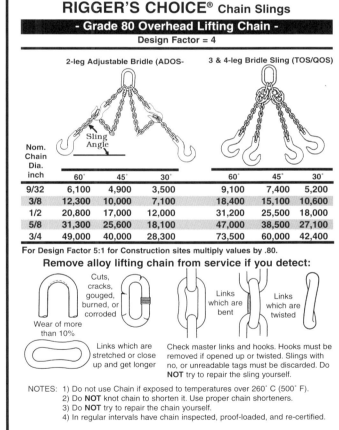

Working Load Limit (WLL): LBS
RIGGER'S CHOICE® Chain Slings
- Grade 80 Overhead Lifting Chain -
Design Factor = 4

Nom. Chain Dia. inch	2-leg Adjustable Bridle (ADOS-			3 & 4-leg Bridle Sling (TOS/QOS)		
	60°	45°	30°	60°	45°	30°
9/32	6,100	4,900	3,500	9,100	7,400	5,200
3/8	12,300	10,000	7,100	18,400	15,100	10,600
1/2	20,800	17,000	12,000	31,200	25,500	18,000
5/8	31,300	25,600	18,100	47,000	38,500	27,100
3/4	49,000	40,000	28,300	73,500	60,000	42,400

For Design Factor 5:1 for Construction sites multiply values by .80.

Remove alloy lifting chain from service if you detect:

Wear of more than 10%

Cuts, cracks, gouged, burned, or corroded

Links which are stretched or close up and get longer

Links which are bent

Links which are twisted

Check master links and hooks. Hooks must be removed if opened up or twisted. Slings with no, or unreadable tags must be discarded. Do **NOT** try to repair the sling yourself.

NOTES: 1) Do not use Chain if exposed to temperatures over 260° C (500° F).
2) Do **NOT** knot chain to shorten it. Use proper chain shorteners.
3) Do **NOT** try to repair the chain yourself.
4) In regular intervals have chain inspected, proof-loaded, and re-certified.

Reprinted with permission from UNIROPE Ltd.

Synthetic Web Slings

Web slings are available in two materials – nylon and polyester (Dacron). Nylon is resistant to many alkalis whereas polyester is resistant to many acids. Consult the manufacturer before using web slings in a chemical environment. Nylon slings are more common but polyester slings are often recommended where headroom is limited since they stretch only half as much as nylon slings.

Synthetic web slings offer a number of advantages for rigging purposes.

– Their relative softness and width create much less tendency to mar or scratch finely machined, highly polished or painted surfaces and less tendency to crush fragile objects than fibre rope, wire rope or chain slings (Figure 35).

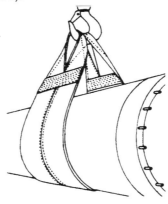

SYNTHETIC WEB SLINGS DO NOT DAMAGE OR CRUSH LOADS
Figure 35

– Because of their flexibility, they tend to mold themselves to the shape of the load (Figure 36).

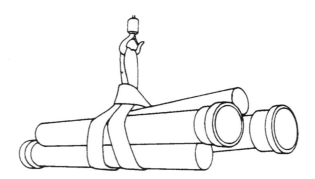

WEB SLINGS MOLD THEMSELVES TO THE LOAD
Figure 36

– They do not rust and thus will not stain ornamental precast concrete or stone.

– They are non-sparking and can be used safely in explosive atmospheres.

– They minimize twisting and spinning during lifting.

– Their light weight permits ease of rigging, their softness precludes hand cuts, and the danger of harm from a free-swinging sling is minimal.

– They are elastic and stretch under load more than either wire rope or chain and can thus absorb heavy shocks and cushion loads. In cases where sling stretching must be minimized, a sling of larger load capacity or a polyester sling should be used.

Synthetic web slings are available in a number of configurations useful in construction.

Endless or Grommet Slings – both ends of one piece of webbing lapped and sewn to form a continuous piece. They can be used as vertical hitches, bridle hitches, in choker arrangements or as basket hitches. Because load contact points can be shifted with every lift, wear is evenly distributed and sling life extended (Figure 37).

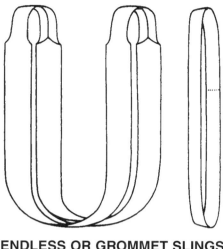

ENDLESS OR GROMMET SLINGS
Figure 37

Standard Eye-and-Eye – webbing assembled and sewn to form a flat body sling with an eye at each end and eye openings in the same plane as the sling body. The eyes may be either full web width or tapered by being folded and sewn narrower than the webbing width (Figure 38).

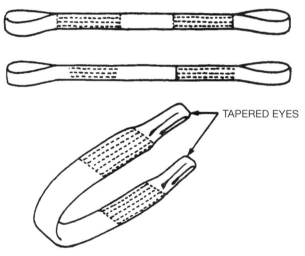

TAPERED EYES

STANDARD EYE-AND-EYE SLINGS
Figure 38

Twisted Eye – an eye-and-eye with twisted terminations at both ends. The eye openings are at 90° to the plane of the sling body. This configuration is available with either full-width or tapered eyes (Figure 39).

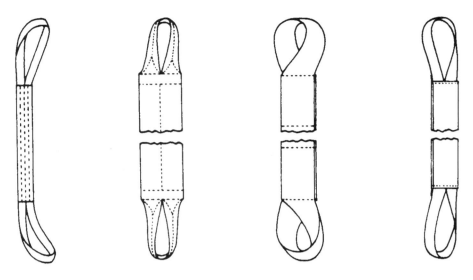

TWISTED EYE SLINGS
Figure 39

In place of sewn eyes, web slings are available with metal end fittings. The most common are triangle and choker hardware. Combination hardware consists of a triangle for one end of the sling and a triangle/rectangle (choker attachment) for the other end. With this arrangement, choker and basket as well as straight hitches may be rigged. Such attachments help reduce wear in the sling eyes and thus lengthen sling life (Figure 40).

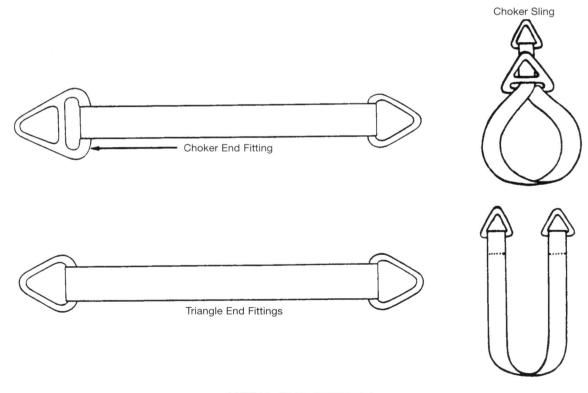

Choker Sling

Choker End Fitting

Triangle End Fittings

METAL END FITTINGS
Figure 40

Despite their inherent toughness, synthetic web slings can be cut by repeated use around sharp-cornered objects and abraded by continually hoisting rough-surfaced loads.

Protective devices offered by most sling manufacturers can minimize these effects.

- **Buffer strips** of leather, nylon, or other materials sewn on the body of the sling protect against wear (Figure 41A). Leather pads are most resistant to wear and cutting, but are subject to weathering and deterioration. They are not recommended in lengths over six feet because their stretch characteristics differ from those of webbing. On the other hand, nylon web wear pads are more resistant to weathering, oils, grease and most alkalis. Moreover they stretch in the same ratio as the sling body.

- **Edge guards** consist of strips of webbing or leather sewn around each edge of the sling (Figure 41B). This is necessary whenever sling edges are subject to damage.

- **Sleeve or sliding tube wear pads** are available for slings used to handle material with sharp edges. The pads are positioned on the sling where required, will not move when the sling stretches, adjust to the load and cover both sides of the sling (Figure 41C).

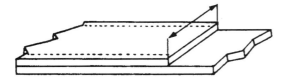

A – REGULAR. This is the type that is sewn on to give fixed protection at expected wear points. They can be sewn anywhere on the sling, at any length on one side or on both sides.

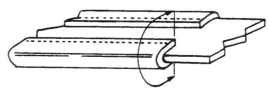

B – EDGE GUARD. A strip of webbing or leather is sewn around each end of the sling. This is necessary for certain applications where the sling edges are subject to damage.

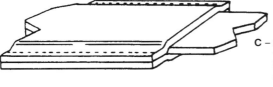

C – SLEEVE. Sometimes called sliding sleeve or tube type wear pads, these pads are ideal for handling material with sharp edges because the sleeve doesn't move when the sling stretches and adjusts to the load. Sleeves cover both sides of the sling and can be shifted to points of expected maximum wear.

WEB SLING
Figure 41

- **Reinforcing strips** sewn into the sling eyes double or triple the eye thickness and greatly increase sling life and safety.

- **Coatings** provide added resistance to abrasion and chemicals as well as a better grip on slippery loads. Coatings can be brightly coloured for safety or load rating.

- **Cotton-faced nylon webbing** affords protection for hoisting granite and other rough-surfaced material.

The rated capacity of synthetic web slings is based on the tensile strength of the webbing, a design factor of 5 and the fabrication efficiency. Fabrication efficiency accounts for loss of strength in the webbing after it is stitched and otherwise modified during manufacture. Fabrication efficiency is typically 80 to 85% for single-ply slings but will be lower for multi-ply slings and very wide slings.

Although manufacturers provide tables for bridle and basket configurations, these should be used with extreme caution. At low sling angles one edge of the web will be overloaded and the sling will tend to tear (Figure 42).

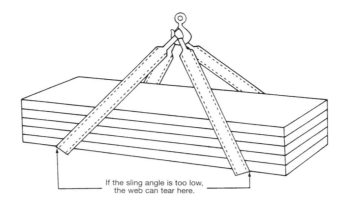

If the sling angle is too low, the web can tear here.

EFFECT OF LOW SLING ANGLE ON WEBBING
Figure 42

Slings with aluminum fittings should never be used in acid or alkali environments. Nylon and polyester slings must not be used at temperatures above 194°F (90°C).

Inspect synthetic web slings regularly. Damage is usually easy to detect. Cuts, holes, tears, frays, broken stitching, worn eyes and worn or distorted fittings, and burns from acid, caustics or heat are immediately evident and signal the need for replacement. Do not attempt repairs yourself.

Synthetic web slings must be labelled to indicate their load rating capacity.

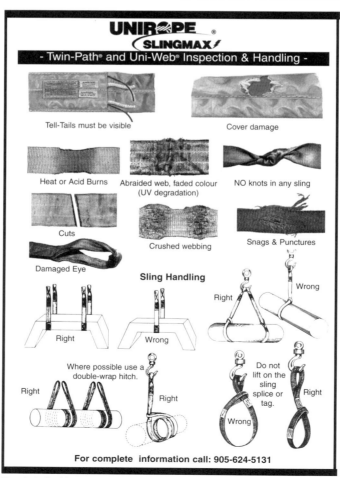

Reprinted with permission from UNIROPE Ltd.

Metal Mesh Slings

Metal mesh slings, also known as wire or chain mesh slings, are well adapted for use where loads are abrasive, hot or tend to cut fabric slings and wire ropes. They resist abrasion and cutting, grip the load firmly without stretching and can withstand temperatures up to 550° (288°C). They have smooth, flat bearing surfaces, conform to irregular shapes, do not kink or tangle and resist corrosion (Figure 43).

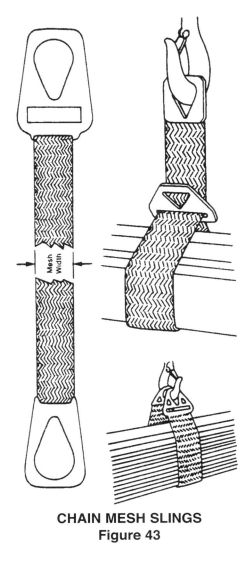

CHAIN MESH SLINGS
Figure 43

For handling loads that would damage the mesh, or for handling loads that the mesh would damage, the slings can be coated with rubber or plastic.

Note that there is no reduction in working load limit for the choker hitch. This is because the hinge action of the mesh prevents any bending of individual wire spirals. Check the manufacturer's rating for the WLL of the specific sling you are using.

Fibre Rope Slings

Fibre rope slings are preferred for some applications because they are pliant, grip the load well and do not mar its surface. They should be used only on light loads, however, and must never be used on objects that have sharp edges capable of cutting the rope or in applications where the sling will be exposed to high temperatures, severe abrasion or acids.

The choice of rope type and size will depend on the application, the weight to be lifted and the sling angle. Before lifting any load with a fibre rope sling, be sure to inspect the sling carefully. Fibre slings, especially manila, deteriorate far more rapidly than wire rope slings and their actual strength is very difficult to estimate.

Like other slings, fibre rope slings should be inspected regularly. Look for external wear and cutting, internal wear between strands, and deterioration of fibres.

Open up the rope by untwisting the strands but take care not to kink them. The inside of the rope should be as bright and clean as when it was new. Check for broken or loose yarns and strands. An accumulation of powder-like dust indicates excessive internal wear between strands as the rope is flexed back and forth during use.

Open Up Rope During Inspections

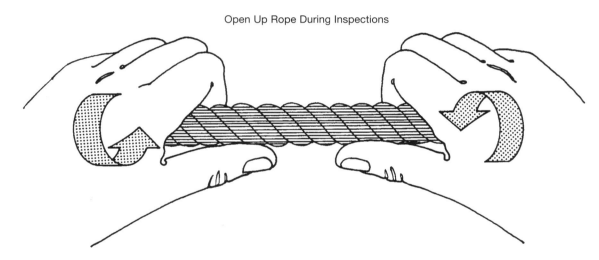

Proper Method of Opening Up the Rope

Rigging Hardware

Know what hardware to use, how to use it, and how its working load limits (WLL) compare with the rope or chain used with it.

All fittings must be of adequate strength for the application. Only forged alloy steel load-rated hardware should be used for overhead lifting. Load-rated hardware is stamped with its WLL (Figure 44).

Inspect hardware regularly and before each lift. Telltale signs include:

– wear

– cracks

– severe corrosion

– deformation/bends

– mismatched parts

– obvious damage.

Figure 44

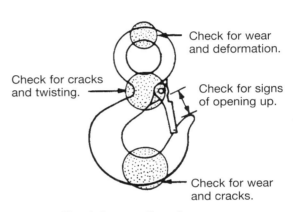

Check for wear and deformation.

Check for cracks and twisting.

Check for signs of opening up.

Check for wear and cracks.

Hook Inspection Areas
Figure 45

Hoisting Hooks

• Should be equipped with safety catches (except for sorting or grab hooks).

• Should be forged alloy steel with WLL stamped or marked on the saddle.

• Should be loaded at the middle of the hook. Applying the load to the tip will load the hook eccentrically and reduce the safe working load considerably.

• Should be inspected regularly and often. Look for wear, cracks, corrosion, and twisting – especially at the tip – and check throat for signs of opening up (Figure 45).

Safety Tip

Whenever two or more ropes are to be placed over a hook, use a shackle to reduce wear and tear on thimble eyes.

Wire Rope Clips

Wire rope clips are widely used for making end terminations. Clips are available in two basic designs: U-bolt and fist grip.

When using U-bolt clips, make sure you have the right type of clip. Forged alloy clips are recommended. Always make certain that U-bolt clips are attached correctly. The U-section must be in contact with the dead end of the rope. Tighten and retighten nuts as required by the manufacturer.

To determine the number of clips and the torque required for specific diameters of rope, refer to Figure 46. For step-by-step instructions on attaching clips, refer to Figure 47.

Clip & rope size inch	Minimum No. of clips	Length of rope to turn back in inches	Required Torque in Ft.Lbs
3/16	2	3-3/4	7.5
1/4	2	4-3/4	15
5/16	2	5-1/4	30
3/8	2	6-1/2	45
7/16	3	7	65
1/2	3	11-1/2	65
9/16	3	12	95
5/8	3	12	95
3/4	4	18	130
7/8	4	19	225
1	5	26	225
1-1/8	6	34	225
1-1/4	7	44	360
1-3/8	7	44	360
1-1/2	8	54	360

Reprinted with permission from UNIROPE Ltd.

Figure 46

72

STEP 1

APPLY FIRST CLIP one base width from dead end of wire rope. U-Bolt over dead end. Live end rests in clip saddle. Tighten nuts evenly to recommended torque.

STEP 2

APPLY SECOND CLIP as close to loop as possible. U-Bolt over dead end. Turn nuts firmly but DO NOT TIGHTEN.

STEP 3

APPLY ALL OTHER CLIPS. Space evenly between first two and 6-7 rope diameters apart.

STEP 4

APPLY TENSION and tighten all nuts to recommended torque.

STEP 5

CHECK NUT TORQUE after rope has been in operation.

Wrong   Right

Figure 47

Swivels

- Reduce bending loads on rigging attachments by allowing the load to orient itself freely.
- Should be used instead of shackles in situations where the shackle may twist and become eccentrically loaded.

Shackles

- Available in various types (Figure 49).
- For hoisting, should be manufactured of forged alloy steel.
- Do not replace shackle pins with bolts (Figure 50). Pins are designed and manufactured to match shackle capacity.
- Check for wear, distortion, and opening up (Figure 51). Check crown regularly for wear. Discard shackles noticeably worn at the crown.
- Do not use a shackle where it will be pulled or loaded at an angle. This severely reduces its capacity and opens up the legs (Figure 52).
- Do not use screw pin shackles if the pin can roll under load and unscrew (Figure 53).

Screw pin anchor shackle

Round pin anchor shackle

Safety type anchor shackle

Screw pin chain shackle

Round pin chain shackle

Safety type chain shackle

Figure 49

Never replace a shackle pin with a bolt

The load will bend the bolt

Figure 50

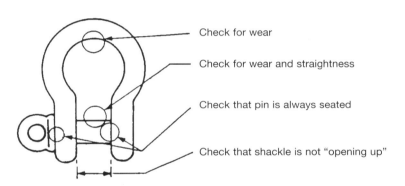

Check for wear

Check for wear and straightness

Check that pin is always seated

Check that shackle is not "opening up"

Figure 51

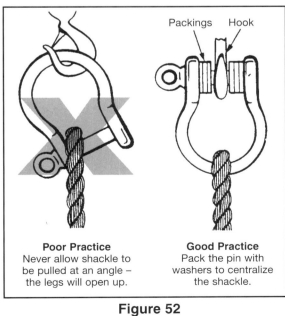

Packings   Hook

Poor Practice
Never allow shackle to be pulled at an angle – the legs will open up.

Good Practice
Pack the pin with washers to centralize the shackle.

Figure 52

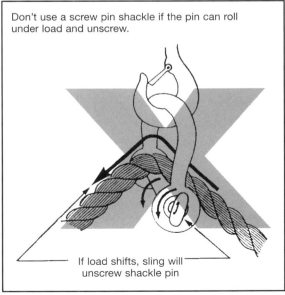

Don't use a screw pin shackle if the pin can roll under load and unscrew.

If load shifts, sling will unscrew shackle pin

Figure 53

Eye Bolts

- For hoisting, use eye or ring bolts of forged alloy steel.

- Use bolts with shoulders or collars. Shoulderless bolts are fine for vertical loading but can bend and lose considerable capacity under angle loading (Figure 54). Even with shoulders, eye and ring bolts lose some capacity when loaded on an angle.

- Make sure that bolts are at right angles to hole, make contact with working surface, and have nuts property torqued (Figure 55).

- Pack bolts with washers when necessary to ensure firm, uniform contact with working surface (Figure 55).

- Make sure that tapped holes for screw bolts are deep enough for uniform grip (Figure 55).

- Apply loads to the plane of the eye, never in the other direction (Figure 55). This is particularly important with bridle slings, which always develop an angular pull in eye bolts unless a spreader bar is used.

- Never insert the point of a hook in an eye bolt. Use a shackle instead (Figure 55).

- Do not reeve a sling through a pair of bolts. Attach a separate sling to each bolt.

Swivel Eye Bolt

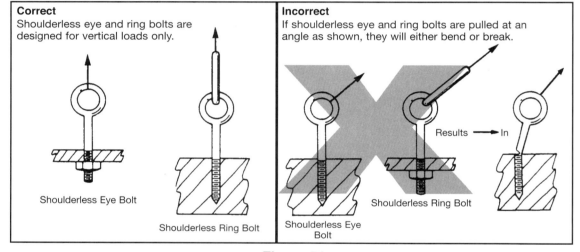

Figure 54

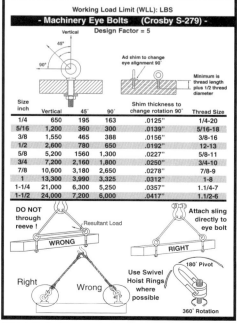

Reprinted with permission from UNIROPE Ltd.

76

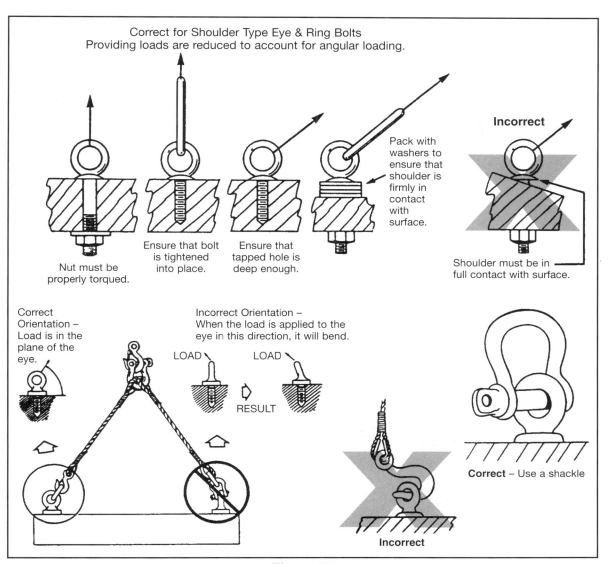

Correct for Shoulder Type Eye & Ring Bolts
Providing loads are reduced to account for angular loading.

Nut must be properly torqued.

Ensure that bolt is tightened into place.

Ensure that tapped hole is deep enough.

Pack with washers to ensure that shoulder is firmly in contact with surface.

Incorrect

Shoulder must be in full contact with surface.

Correct Orientation – Load is in the plane of the eye.

Incorrect Orientation – When the load is applied to the eye in this direction, it will bend.

LOAD   LOAD

RESULT

Correct – Use a shackle

Incorrect

Figure 55

Snatch Blocks

- A single or multi-sheave block that opens on one side so a rope can be slipped over the sheave rather than threaded through the block (Figure 56).

- Available with hook, shackle, eye, and swivel end fittings.

- Normally used when it's necessary to change the direction of pull on a line. Stress on the snatch block varies tremendously with the angle between the lead and load lines. With both lines parallel, 1000 pounds on the lead line results in 2000 pounds on the block, hook, and anchorage. As the angle between the lines increases, the stress is reduced (Figure 57).

- To determine the load on block, hook, and anchorage, multiply the pull on the lead line or the weight of the load being lifted by a suitable factor from the table in Figure 19.33 and add 10% for sheave friction.

When Open

Figure 56

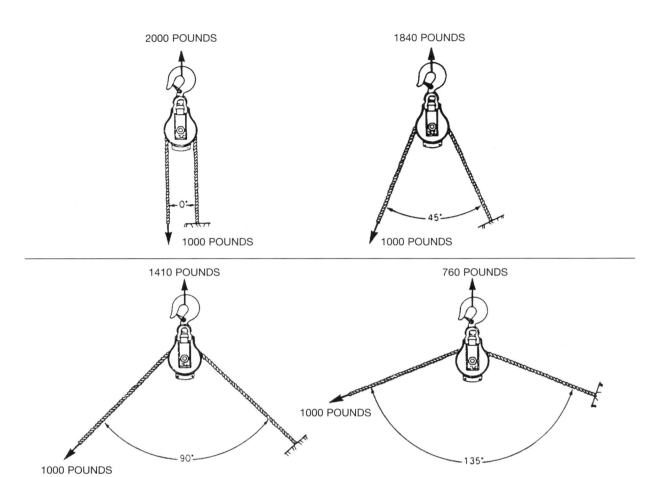

Figure 57

MULTIPLICATION FACTORS FOR SNATCH BLOCK LOADS	
Angle Between Lead and Load Lines	Multiplication Factor
10°	1.99
20°	1.97
30°	1.93
40°	1.87
45°	1.84
50°	1.81
60°	1.73
70°	1.64
80°	1.53
90°	1.41
100°	1.29
110°	1.15
120°	1.00
130°	.84
135°	.76
140°	.68
150°	.52
160°	.35
170°	.17
180°	.00

Turnbuckles

- Can be supplied with eye end fittings, hook end fittings, jaw end fittings, stub end fittings, and any combination of these (Figure 58).

- Rated loads are based on the outside diameter of the threaded portion of the end fitting and on the type of end fitting. Jaw, eye, and stub types are rated equally; hook types are rated lower.

- Should be weldless alloy steel.

- When turnbuckles are exposed to vibration, lock frames to end fittings. This will prevent turning and loosening. Use wire or manufacturer-supplied lock nuts to prevent turning (Figure 59).

- When tightening a turnbuckle, do not apply, more torque than you would to a bolt of equal size.

- Inspect turnbuckles frequently for cracks in end fittings (especially at the neck of the shank), deformed end fittings, deformed and bent rods and bodies, cracks and bends around the internally threaded portion, and signs of thread damage.

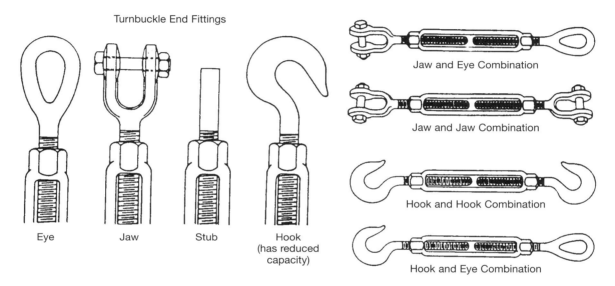

Turnbuckle End Fittings

Eye   Jaw   Stub   Hook (has reduced capacity)

Jaw and Eye Combination

Jaw and Jaw Combination

Hook and Hook Combination

Hook and Eye Combination

Figure 58

Manufacturer-supplied lock nut   Wire

Figure 59

Table 8 gives the working load limits for turnbuckles based on the diameter of the shank. Note how the use of hook end fittings reduces capacity.

Table 8
Turnbuckle Types and Capacities

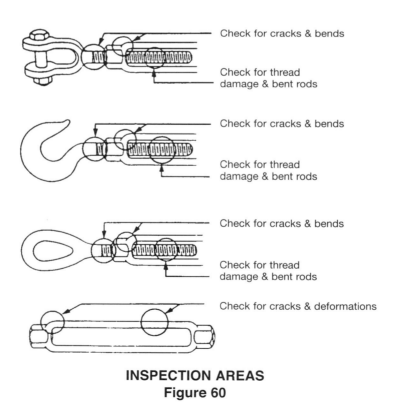

Size & Thread dia.	WLL with Jaw or Eye lbs	WLL with Hook lbs	Available Take-Up sizes inch
1/4	500	400	4
5/16	800	700	4-1/2
3/8	1,200	1,000	6
1/2	2,200	1,500	6,9,12
5/8	3,500	2,250	6,9,12
3/4	5,200	3,000	6,9,12,18
7/8	7,200	4,000	12,18
1	10,000	5,000	6,12,18,24
1-1/4	15,200	6,500	12,18,24
1-1/2	21,400	7,500	12,18,24

Jaw & Eye - use Jaw or Eye WLL

Jaw & Jaw - use Jaw or Eye WLL

Hook & Jaw - use Hook WLL

Hook & Eye - use Hook WLL

Reprinted with permission from UNIROPE Ltd.

Figure 60 shows the areas of a turnbuckle that require special attention during inspection.

Check for cracks & bends

Check for thread damage & bent rods

Check for cracks & bends

Check for thread damage & bent rods

Check for cracks & bends

Check for thread damage & bent rods

Check for cracks & deformations

INSPECTION AREAS
Figure 60

Spreader and Equalizer Beams

Spreader beams are usually used to support long loads during lifts. They eliminate the hazard of the load tipping, sliding, or bending as well as the possibility of low sling angles and the tendency of the slings to crush the load.

Equalizer beams are used to equalize the load in sling legs and to keep equal loads on dual hoist lines when making tandem lifts.

Spreader and equalizer beams are both normally fabricated to suit a specific application. If a beam is to be used which has not been designed for the application, make sure that it has adequate width, depth, length, and material.

The capacity of beams with multiple attachment points depends on the distance between the points. For example, if the distance between attachment points is doubled, the capacity of the beam is cut in half.

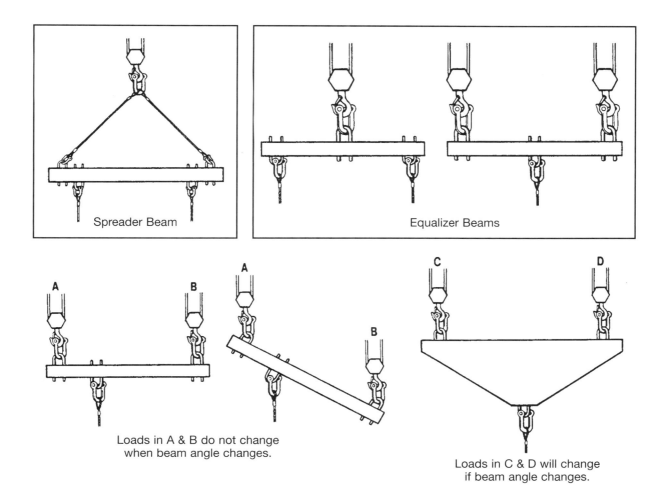

Spreader Beam

Equalizer Beams

Loads in A & B do not change
when beam angle changes.

Loads in C & D will change
if beam angle changes.

Hoisting Tips

- Never wrap a wire rope sling completely around a hook. The tight radius will damage the sling.
- Make sure the load is balanced in the hook. Eccentric loading can reduce capacity dangerously (Figure 61).

Point Loading

CAPACITY IS SEVERELY REDUCED
Figure 61

- Never point-load a hook unless it is designed and rated for such use. Point-loading can cut capacity by more than half.
- Never wrap the crane hoist rope around the load. Attach the load to the crane hook by slings or other rigging devices.
- Avoid bending wire rope slings near attached fittings or at eye sections.

Section 4

Rigging Tools and Devices

- Jacks (ratchet, hydraulic)
- Blocking and Cribbing
- Rollers
- Inclined Planes
- Lever-Operated Hoists
- Chain Hoists
- Grip-Action Hoists (Tirfors)
- Electric Hoists and Pendant Cranes
- Winches
- Anchorage Points

Section 4

Rigging Tools and Devices

The *Regulations for Construction Projects* require that an inspection and maintenance program be implemented to ensure that rigging equipment is kept in safe condition. Procedures must ensure that inspection and maintenance have not only been carried out but have been duly recorded.

Rigging operations often involve the use of various tools and devices such as jacks, rollers, hoists, and winches. Each has its own unique features, uses, and requirements for safe operation and maintenance.

The construction regulations also require that the manufacturer's operating instructions for such tools and devices be available on site. The rigger must read and follow all of these instructions to operate and maintain the equipment properly. The rigger must also read any warning information which may be stamped, printed, tagged, or attached to the rigging device.

This section identifies some of the commonly used rigging tools and devices and explains procedures for their safe operation and maintenance. For more detailed information, see the Jacks and Rollers chapter in *Specialized Rigging (DS035).*

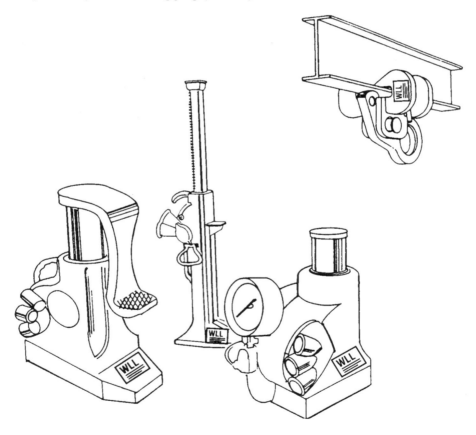

Jacks

While there are a great many types of jacks, the ratchet jack and heavy duty hydraulic jack are the two types most commonly used in construction.

Ratchet jacks are usually limited to capacities under 20 tons because of the physical effort required to raise such a load. They do, however, have a much longer travel than hydraulic jacks and can therefore lift loads higher without having to re-block. Most ratchet jacks have a foot lift or "toe" near the base to lift loads which are close to the ground. Lifts can be made from the "head" or the "toe" of the jack. These jacks are often called toe jacks or track jacks (Figure 1).

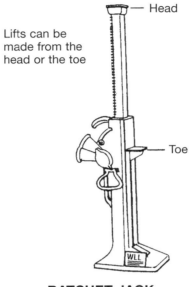

Head

Lifts can be
made from the
head or the toe

Toe

WLL

RATCHET JACK
Figure 1

Do not use extensions or "cheaters" on the handles supplied with ratchet jacks. If cheaters are necessary the jack is overloaded.

Hydraulic jacks are very popular in construction because they are quite compact and can lift very heavy loads. They are readily available in capacities ranging from a few tons to 100 tons. Some specialty units have capacities up to 1,000 tons. Lift heights are usually limited to approximately 8 inches or less but some can go as high as 36 inches (Figure 2).

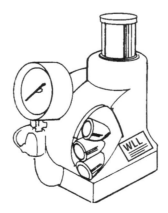

WLL

SELF-CONTAINED HYDRAULIC JACK
Figure 2

Hydraulic jacks are also available in low profile models that can be positioned under a load close to the ground (Figure 3). Also known as "button jacks", these are useful for lifting a load high enough to get a regular jack in place.

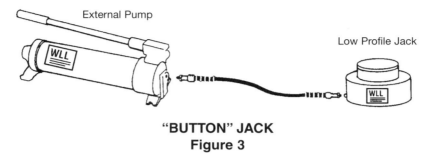

External Pump

Low Profile Jack

"BUTTON" JACK
Figure 3

Like ratchet jacks, hydraulic jacks are available with toe lifts (Figure 4).

HYDRAULIC JACK WITH TOE LIFT
Figure 4

The pumps powering hydraulic jacks may be contained in the jacks or be separate external power units. Separate units may be hand-operated or electrically powered, but the self-contained pumps are always hand-operated.

With all types of hydraulic jacks it is critical that no further force be applied after the ram has run its full travel. The resultant high pressure in the hydraulic fluid can damage the seals and, in the case of external power units, burst the hoses.

Most external power units are equipped, however, with pressure relief valves. At the factory one valve will be set at the absolute maximum pressure while another will be adjustable to lower settings by the user. Make sure you are familiar with the operation of this safety feature.

Most hydraulic jacks can be fitted with a gauge on the housing or at the pump to monitor hydraulic pressure. When used with a given jack, the gauges can be calibrated to measure the approximate load on the unit.

Hoses connecting pumps to jacks require careful attention. Make sure they are free of kinks and cracks. Check the couplings, especially at the crimp. This area is prone to cracking and is often the weak link in the hose assembly. Threads should also be checked for damage, wear, cross-threading and tightness. Remember that these hoses have to withstand pressures up to 10,000 psi.

Don't use hoses that are unnecessarily long. Shorter hoses will leave the area less congested and reduce the chance of accidental damage.

The handles on jacks or hand-operated pump units are designed so that the rated capacity and pressure can be obtained with little physical effort. Don't use extensions or "cheaters" on the handles. Again, if the load can't be raised with the handle supplied the jack is overloaded.

Jacks should only be used in a true vertical position for lifting. Otherwise side-loading can cause the piston to rub against the housing. If this happens, the piston will be scored and allow fluid to leak at the seal which may cause the jack to slip.

Be extremely careful when using hydraulic jacks in welding areas or around corrosive chemicals. Sparks or acids can cause pitting on the ram or damage hoses.

Hydraulic jacks are generally not equipped with check valves. But check valves can be installed in the hoses of an external pump and are recommended. Alternatively, some hydraulic jacks have retaining nuts that can be screwed against the housing to hold the load for a short time.

Jacks should never be used for long-term support of a load. Blocking is much more stable and safe. Whenever possible, the load should be progressively blocked as jacking proceeds. This will allow for the unexpected.

Always jack loads one end at a time. Never jack loads one side at a time as this will be far less stable than jacking the ends.

If it is necessary to work or even reach under a load on jacks, place safety blocking under the load as a precaution.

Make sure timbers used for blocking or cribbing are long enough to distribute the load over a large enough area and provide sufficient stability. Crib height should not exceed the length of timbers used.

All jacks should be thoroughly inspected periodically, depending on how they are used. For regular use at one location they should be inspected every six months or more frequently if the lifts approach capacity. Jacks sent out for special jobs should be inspected when received and when returned. Jacks subjected to high loads or shock should be inspected immediately.

Because jack bases are relatively small, care must be taken to ensure that the floor or ground can withstand the high pressures often associated with jacking operations. Blocking or matting under the jacks will distribute the load over a greater area and reduce bearing pressure.

Jacks – Inspection

Whether ratchet or hydraulic, all jacks should be inspected before each shift or use. Check for:

- improper engagement or extreme wear of pawl and rack
- cracked or broken rack teeth
- cracked or damaged plunger
- leaking hydraulic fluid
- scored or damaged plunger
- swivel heads and caps that don't function properly
- damaged or improperly assembled accessory equipment

Remember: When using jacks, always try to block as you go. Never use jacks for long-term support. Block properly instead.

Blocking and Cribbing

Blocking or cribbing must

- be sufficient to support load
- be set on firm, level ground or floor
- be close together
- be dry and free of grease
- be stacked no higher than the length of the timbers used
- follow the jacking process
- distribute load over enough area to provide stability.

Note: In some cases, solid blocking may be required.

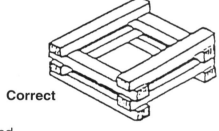

Correct

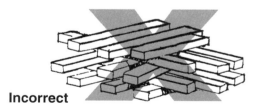

Incorrect

Rollers

Rollers can be used for moving loads horizontally or on slight inclines, provided the surface is firm and even. Rollers may be aluminum or steel round stock, heavy steel pipe, or a manufactured caster unit (Figure 5).

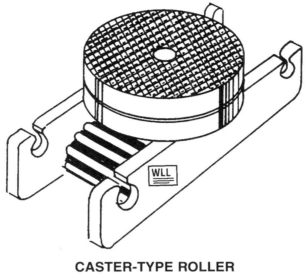

CASTER-TYPE ROLLER
Figure 5

Cylinder rollers are useful for short distances or where the load will have to negotiate corners. The rollers can be placed on angles to swing the ends of the load, allowing turns in tight areas (Figure 6).

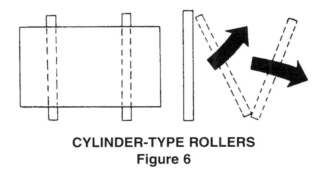

CYLINDER-TYPE ROLLERS
Figure 6

Cylinder rollers should be round, true and smooth to minimize the force required to move the load. Caster rollers can be supplied in a number of configurations for flat surfaces, tracks, I-beams or channels. They create very little friction and allow heavy loads to be moved with little force. In fact, the rigger may sometimes require more friction to provide an extra measure of control.

The most important aspect in rolling is control of the load. Make sure that all equipment including slings and hardware is sufficient to handle the loads that will be developed at each stage of the operation. Always attach a second means of restraint such as a tirfor or winch to the load to allow for the unexpected. The possibility of shock loads should be considered when sizing winches or tirfors for back-up protection.

Check the condition of floors or ground before using rollers. Bearing pressure can be reduced by using more rollers and large steel or aluminum plate to distribute the load. Make sure the joints in the plates or skids are staggered. It is often necessary to assess the structure supporting floors. Temporary shoring may be necessary.

Inclined Planes

The method used to calculate the required pull up an incline is only approximate. Though widely used because of its simplicity, the method yields values higher than the actual force required. The formula is more accurate for slight inclines (1:5) than steep inclines (1:1). Table 1 shows the difference between the actual pull required and the pull calculated with friction of 5%.

TABLE 1

Actual Force versus Force Calculated by Simplified Method with 5% Friction	
	Simplified Method F = .250W Actual Force F = .245W Error: 2%
	Simplified Method F = .383W Actual Force F = .364W Error: 5%
	Simplified Method F = .550W Actual Force F = .492W Error: 12%
	Simplified Method F = 1.05W Actual Force F = .742W Error: 42%

For most applications the simplified method is adequate because the value used for friction is itself only approximate.

Formula (5% Friction)

$F = W \times H/L + .05W$

where

F = Required Force
H = Height
L = Length
W = Weight of Load

Table 2 lists some examples of approximate coefficients of friction. Note that some of the combinations of materials have a considerable range of values.

TABLE 2

Examples of Friction Coefficients	
Steel on Steel	40-60%
Leather on Metal	60%
Wood on Stone	40%
Iron on Stone	30-70%
Grease Plates	15%
Load on Wheels or Rollers	2-5%

Lever-Operated Hoists or Come-Alongs

Come-alongs are a very portable means of lifting or pulling loads short distances. They can be used vertically, horizontally or on an angle. Otherwise all points covered in the section on chain hoists apply equally to come-alongs.

A come-along that requires the use of a cheater or the help of another worker to move a load is inadequate for the job. Use a come-along with a larger capacity.

Lever-Operated Hoist – Safety Precautions

- Inspect for defects.
- Do not use cheater on hoist handle.
- Do not overload. Working load limit (WLL) should be marked on device.
- Do not apply the load to the tip of the hook.
- Do not use the hoist chain as a sling or choker.
- Make sure of your footing before operating the hoist.
- Do not leave the suspended load unattended.
- Keep hoist chain straight.
- Stand clear of load and pulling path of hoist chain.
- Keep upper and lower hooks in a straight line so that the frame is free to swivel.
- Do not use a hoist with a twisted, kinked, damaged, or worn chain.
- Ensure that anchorage and structure will support the load.

CHAIN HOISTS

Chain hoists are useful because the load can be stopped and kept stationary at any point. Because of their slow rate of travel, chain hoists also allow precise vertical placement.

Chain hoists should be rigged so that there is a straight line between the upper and lower hooks. They are intended for use in a vertical or near vertical position only. If rigged at an angle, the upper hook can be damaged at the shank and the throat may open up. If the gear housing is resting against an object while under load it can be damaged or broken (Figure 10).

Always make sure that the hoist is hanging freely.

Before using the hoist, inspect the chain for nicks, gouges, twists, and wear. Check the chain guide for wear. Hooks should be measured for signs of opening up. Ensure that the hooks swivel freely and are equipped with safety catches. If the hoist has been subjected to shock loads or dropped, it should be inspected thoroughly before being put back in service. Check the load brake by raising the load a couple of inches off the ground and watching for creep.

If the hoist chain requires replacement, follow the manufacturer's recommendations. Different manufacturers use different pitches for their load chain. Chain intended for one brand of hoist will not mesh properly with the lift wheel of another brand and the hoist will not operate properly, if at all.

The load chain on chain hoists is case-hardened to reduce surface wear and is unsuitable for any other use. Load chain will stretch 3% before failing, whereas Grade 8 alloy chain will stretch at least 15%. Load chains are too brittle for any other application. Any load chain removed from a hoist should be destroyed by cutting it into short pieces. Never try to repair a load chain yourself. Welding will destroy the heat treatment of the chain entirely.

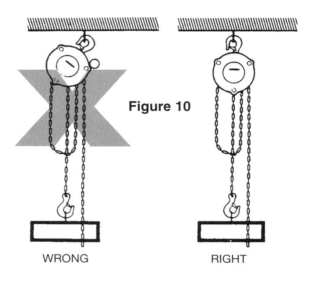

Figure 10

WRONG   RIGHT

Chain Hoist – Safety Precautions
- Inspect for wear and damage regularly.
- Do not overload.
- Do not leave a suspended load unattended.
- Do not stand under the load.
- Do not use the hoist chain as a sling or choker.
- Do not apply the load to the tip of the hook.
- Avoid hoisting on angles.
- Chain hoists must be used in the vertical position.
- Only one operator should pull on a single hand chain at one time.
- Ensure that load chain is properly seated in wheels or sprockets before lifting.
- Ensure that anchorage and structure will support the load.
- Maintain the chain hoist according to manufacturer's specifications.

Grip Action Hoists or Tirfors

Grip-action hoists, commonly known by the trade name Tirfor, are useful for long lifts or pulls since they act on a continuous length of wire rope. Like the come-along, they can be used in any orientation. The tirfor can draw rope through the unit, as a come-along draws chain, or pull itself along a fixed rope, as on a swingstage (Figure 11).

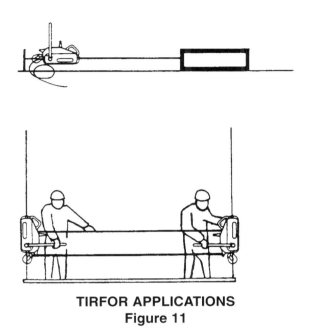

TIRFOR APPLICATIONS
Figure 11

Tirfors are available with capacities ranging from 3/4 to 3½ tons. The rope can be reeved through a block system to gain mechanical advantage and increase the capacity of the unit.

Tirfors are operated by two levers – one for forward motion, the other for reverse. The levers operate two jaws which alternately grip and draw the rope through the unit. Figure 12 illustrates the action of the jaws on the rope. A third lever releases both jaws to allow rope to be installed, tensioned, or disengaged.

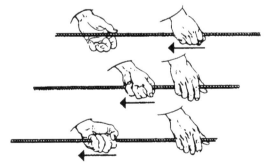

THE TIRFOR PRINCIPLE
Figure 12

Tirfors can be fitted with hydraulic rams to operate the levers. Up to four units can be operated simultaneously from a single hydraulic power supply (Figure 13).

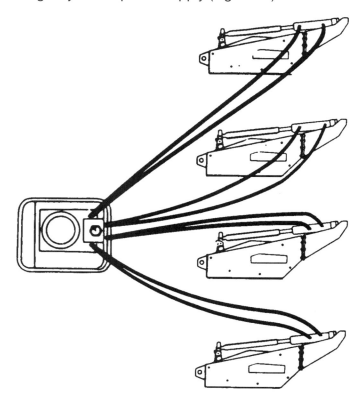

HYDRAULICALLY ACTUATED TIRFORS WITH COMMON POWER SOURCE
Figure 13

Another type of grip-action hoist uses discs to clamp and drive the rope in a continuous motion (Figure 14). These are available with electric, air, or hydraulic motors. Disc type hoists provide greater rope speed but less capacity than the jaw type.

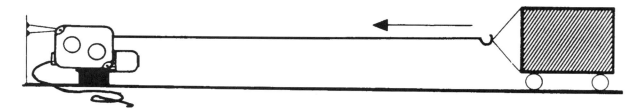

DISC-TYPE HOIST OR PULLER
Figure 14

Tirfor ropes are specifically designed for the clamping and pulling forces applied to them. The ropes are galvanized and unlubricated and have very tight diameter tolerance. No other rope should ever be used on tirfors.

Handle tirfor rope carefully to ensure that it does not kink. Kinked rope will jam in the mechanism and prevent the rope from passing through the hoist. Ropes must be kept free from dirt and oil to ensure smooth, safe operation.

Like chain falls and come-alongs tirfors should be tested under load to ensure that the unit functions properly in both directions and that there is no slippage.

Electric Wire Rope Hoists, Electric Chain Hoists, Pendant Cranes

Electric wire rope and electric chain hoists may be suspended from a fixed point or a trolley. The trolley may be motorized but very often the hoist is moved by tugging gently on the pendant. These units can only move along a fixed straight line (beam).

Pendant cranes, on the other hand, trolley along a bridge (east-west) which travels on rails (north-south). Pendant cranes have greater capacity than the other hoists and usually have two or more parts of line.

Apart from these differences, the devices are quite similar in operating procedures and precautions. Hoist operators must adhere to the following points.

- Know and never exceed the working load limit of the hoisting equipment.
- Ensure that controls work properly without excessive play, delay or effort.
- Check pendant control cable for cuts, kinking, or signs of wear.
- Check hoist cables for fraying, kinking, crushing, and twisting between the cable and the drum.
- Look at the hoist drum for proper alignment and stacking of the cable.
- Inspect the hook for cracks, bending, or distortion, and the safety latch for proper operation.
- Don't try to lengthen or repair the load chain or rope.
- Read and follow manufacturer's instructions and all instructions and warnings on the hoist.
- Position the hoist directly over the load.
- After the hook is placed in the lifting ring, apply slight pressure to the hoist to ensure that the lifting ring is seated in the bottom of the hook and that the hook is properly aligned.
- Between lifts, check whether the rope is properly seated on the drum.
- Ensure that the intended path of travel is clear of people and obstructions and that the intended destination is ready to receive the load.
- Check brakes for excessive drift.
- Ensure proper clearance for movement.
- Position yourself on the pendant side of the hoist to get maximum clearance from the load and to prevent entanglement of cables.
- Avoid sudden starts, stops, or reverses.
- Raise the load only high enough to avoid obstructions.
- Do not hoist loads over workers; wait until the area is vacated.
- Be alert for any variation in hoist operation and any possible malfunction.
- Do not leave a load suspended in the air. If a short delay is unavoidable, lock the controls.
- Do not allow unqualified personnel to operate hoists.
- Never operate hoist to extreme limits of chain or rope.
- Avoid sharp contact between two hoists, between hoist and end post, and between hooks and hoist body.
- Never use the hoist rope or chain as a sling.
- Never use chain or rope as a ground for welding or touch a live welding electrode to the chain or rope.
- Avoid swinging the load or hook when travelling the hoist.
- Pull in a straight line so that neither hoist body, load chain nor rope is angled around anything.

Some hoists are equipped with limit switches. Generally these devices stop the wind automatically at its maximum allowable up position, down position and travel limits (if rail-mounted). Check limit switches daily for correct operation.

Whenever the operator does not have a clear view of the load and its intended path of travel, a signaller must direct operations. Signals for pendant cranes differ from those for mobile and tower cranes since machine movements are different (Figure 15). Make sure that everyone involved knows the signals required for pendant cranes.

STOP. Arm extended, palm down, move hand right and left.

DOG EVERYTHING. Clasp hands in front of body.

MOVE SLOWLY. Use one hand to give any motion signal and place other hand motionless in front of hand, giving the motion signal. (HOIST SLOWLY SHOWN AS EXAMPLE).

HOIST. With forearm vertical, forefinger pointing up, move hand in small horizontal circles.

LOWER. With arm extended downward, fore–finger pointing down, move hand in small horizontal circles.

MULTIPLE TROLLEYS. Hold up one finger for block marked "1", and two fingers for block marked "2". Regular signals follow.

TRAVEL. Arm extended forward, hands open and slightly raised, making pushing motion in direction of travel.

TROLLEY TRAVEL. Palm up, fingers closed, thumb pointing in direction of motion, jerk hand horizontally.

SIGNALS FOR PENDANT CRANES

Figure 15

Winches

Base-mounted winches, or tuggers, are a compact, versatile tool for many hoisting and rigging operations (for more detailed information, see the Tuggers chapter in *Specialized Rigging—DS035*). They are particularly useful in areas not accessible to mobile cranes or where there is not enough headroom for a crane to operate. Figure 16 shows a tugger and snatch block arrangement for hoisting. Make sure that the rope leaves the drum at a downward angle and that the loose end is securely anchored.

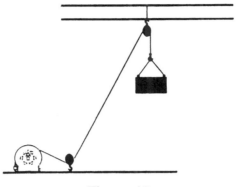

Figure 16

The forces on snatch blocks and their anchorage points depend on the angle by which the direction of pull is changed. The diagrams below indicate how snatch block loads vary with rope angle.

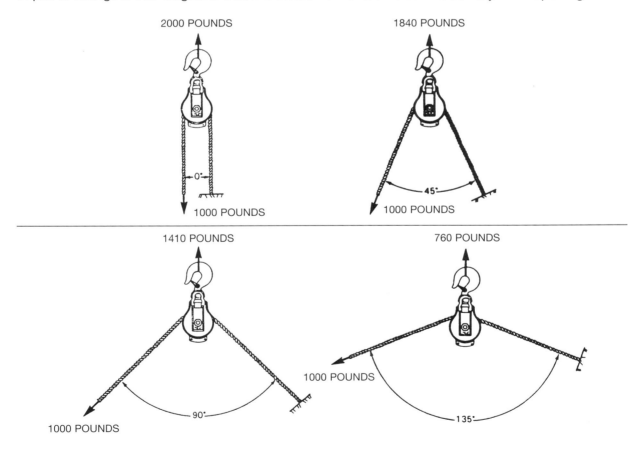

Wire rope used on tuggers should have an independent wire rope core to resist crushing as it is compressed by successive layers of rope on the drum.

Anchorage Points

Hoists, winches, tirfors, and other rigging devices require secure anchorage points. Anchors may be overhead, in the floor, or at lateral points in walls or other structures. The arrangement may involve columns, beams, beam clamps, welded lugs, slings, or block and tackle. Whatever the method, riggers must be certain of the loads involved and the anchorage required.

Load on Structure

The following examples illustrate how to calculate the load on the structure in two typical applications.

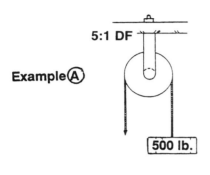

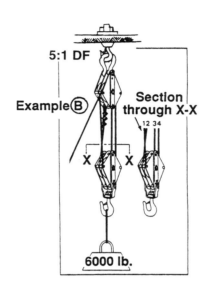

Lead Line Load	=	Load + Parts of Line at Load
Lead Line Load A	=	500 ÷ 1
	=	500 lb
Lead Line Load B	=	6000 ÷ 4
	=	1500 lb

Load on Structure	=	Load + Lead Line Load
Load on Structure A	=	500 + 500
	=	1000 lb
Load on Structure B	=	6000 + 1500
	=	7500 lb

98

Columns

Columns are generally not designed to withstand significant lateral forces. Anchorage points should be placed at the base, near a connection to a beam or other lateral support (Figure 1). Because the member is already in compression, the effect of a small deflection is amplified and the column could buckle.

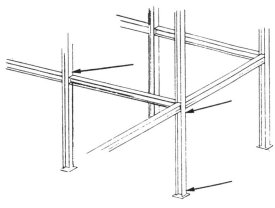

ANCHOR PLACEMENT ON COLUMNS
Figure 1

Beams

Load beams near column or other vertical support points to minimize bending (Figure 2). If the beam is an I section, it may be necessary to weld stiffeners to the web to withstand the additional shear force applied (Figure 3).

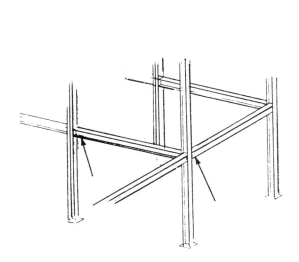

ANCHOR PLACEMENT ON BEAMS
Figure 2

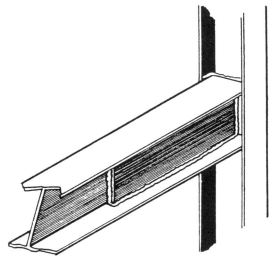

WEB STIFFENER
Figure 3

Beam Clamps

Beam clamps provide a very secure anchorage point if used correctly. They are commonly available with capacities up to 12 tons and have various jaw widths. Figure 5 shows different types.

The jaws are usually designed for a range of flange widths. For example, one clamp might fit flanges 4½" to 9" wide. Clamps should never be used on flanges outside the range specified as they will not afford sufficient grip on the member.

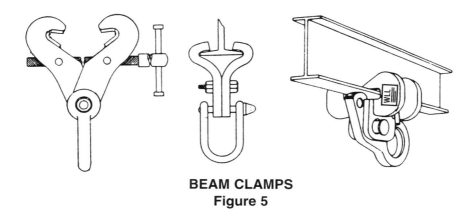

BEAM CLAMPS
Figure 5

Most beam clamps are designed for use at 90° to the flange. For applications requiring an angle loading, make sure that the clamp is designed for it and that the beam can withstand it (Figure 6).

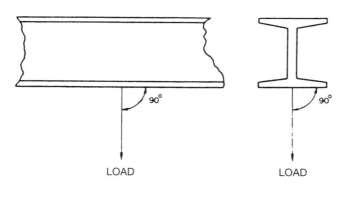

IN LINE LOADING
Figure 6

Be particularly careful that the load does not deform the flange. This is most likely to occur with light sections where the flange is wide and thin.

Beam clamps should be centred on the flange and properly seated.

Manufacturers are required to mark beam clamps with working load limits. But the ratings apply only to the clamps. The capacity of the beam must be evaluated separately.

Slings

Slings are a common method of anchoring equipment to a structure. The double wrap basket hitch is the preferred method since the load in the sling is shared on two legs and the double wrap distributes the load on the member. It is also less prone to slippage than a single choker or single basket hitch. Make sure that the sling is long enough to avoid sharp angles in the legs (Figure 7).

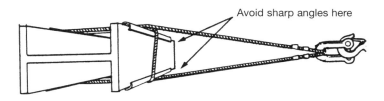

LASHING AROUND COLUMN OR BEAM
Figure 7

The use of softeners will protect the member and the sling from damage and increase the radius of bending in the sling. Figure 8 shows how strength diminishes as wire rope is bent around smaller and smaller diameters.

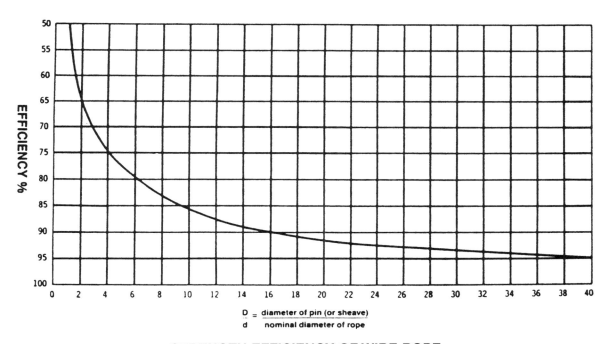

$$\frac{D}{d} = \frac{\text{diameter of pin (or sheave)}}{\text{nominal diameter of rope}}$$

STRENGTH EFFICIENCY OF WIRE ROPE
WHEN BENT OVER PINS OR SHEAVES OF VARIOUS SIZES
Figure 8

Welded Lugs

Lugs welded to a beam or column must be compatible with the member in metallic composition. The appropriate welding rod must also be used. The lug should be welded on the centre line of the flange, in line with the web (Figure 9). Keep loading in line with the lug. Avoid side loading.

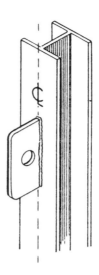

LUG PLACEMENT ON ɪ SECTION
Figure 9

Whatever the method of attachment, it is important to realize that the structure is usually not designed for the additional loads applied. The only way to be sure is through evaluation by a structural engineer.

Section 5

Introduction to Crane Operations

- ■ **Responsibilities**
- ■ **Basic Types and Configurations**
- ■ **Hazards in Crane Operating Areas**
- ■ **Working near Powerlines**
- ■ **Factors Affecting Crane Capacity**
- ■ **Setup Summary**
- ■ **Machine Selection**
- ■ **Signalling**

Section 5

Introduction to Crane Operations

Crane operation carries with it a greater potential for disaster than nearly any other activity on a construction project. Crane accidents are often the most costly construction accidents when measured either in lives or in dollars. All personnel involved in crane operations must understand their jobs, their responsibilities, and their part in the overall safety of each lift.

Preparation begins with a clear definition of responsibilities. No single set of guidelines can cover every detail of the many different types of crane operations. But this section spells out primary responsibilities for the major parties involved – owners, operators, site supervision, and workers.

Responsibilities entail knowledge. Riggers must be trained and experienced. They must know how to:

- establish weights
- judge distances, heights, and clearances
- select tackle and hardware suitable to the load
- rig the load safely.

Signallers must be competent and capable of directing the crane and load to ensure safe, efficient operation. Knowledge of the hand signals for hoisting is a must, as it is for operators.

The crane operator is generally responsible for the safety of the operation as soon as the load is lifted clear of the ground. Whenever there is reasonable cause to believe that the lift may be dangerous or unsafe, the operator must refuse to proceed until the concern has been reported to the supervisor, any hazard has been corrected, and safe conditions have been confirmed.

This section includes information of use to riggers, operators, and others involved either directly or indirectly in crane operations. The information covers major responsibilities, hazards and safeguards in crane operating areas, factors that affect crane capacity, pinch points and other hazards around equipment, considerations for safe setup, requirements for providing signallers, and the international hand signals for hoisting.

Responsibilities

Crane Owner

The crane owner must ensure that
- safe, suitable equipment is provided to meet the requirements of the job

- operators are capable and aware of their responsibilities

- maintenance, repair, transport, assembly, and other personnel are trained and experienced to handle their specific jobs

- training and upgrading are provided for all personnel

- responsibilities and authority are clearly designated for each crew

- a thorough equipment maintenance and inspection program is in operation, including logbooks and other required documentation

- client and site supervision are capable and aware of their responsibilities

- equipment is maintained and inspected in accordance with manufacturer's requirements and applicable regulations.

Operator

The operator is generally responsible for the safety of the crane operation as soon as the load is lifted. Operators must know:

- the particular model of crane they operate, its characteristics, functions, and limitations

- the information in the crane's operating manual

- the crane's load chart, including all notes and warnings, and how to calculate or determine the crane's actual net capacity in every possible configuration

- proper inspection and maintenance procedures to be followed in accordance with the guidelines of manufacturer and owner

- any site conditions that may affect crane operation, including the presence of overhead powerlines

- basic load rigging procedures.

In addition, the Operator must:

- inform the owner, in writing, of any problems with the machine, preferably in the machine's logbook

- record in the logbook all inspection, maintenance, and work done on the crane in the field

- check that the site is properly prepared for crane operation

- review plans and requirements with site supervision

- find out the load and rigging weight and where the load is to be placed.

[Although operators are NOT responsible for determining load weights, they become responsible if they do so or if they lift the load without checking the weight with site supervision.]

- determine the number of parts of hoist line required
- check the load chart to ensure that the crane has enough net capacity for each planned lift
- select the best boom, jib, and crane configuration to suit load, site, and lift conditions
- assume responsibility for assembling, setting up, and rigging the crane properly
- follow the manufacturer's operating instructions in accordance with the load chart
- consider all factors that may reduce crane capacity and adjust the load weight accordingly
- maintain communication with signallers
- ensure that the oiler is in a safe place during operation
- operate in a smooth, controlled, and safe manner
- shut down and secure the machine properly when leaving it unattended.

Site Supervision

Site supervision (foreman, rigger foreman, lead hand of the trade involved, etc.) has overall responsibility for the lift and must therefore plan all phases of the operation. Specifically, site supervisors must:

- supervise all work involving the crane
- determine the correct load weight and radius and inform the operator
- ensure that the rigging crew is experienced and capable of establishing weights; judging distances, heights, and clearances; selecting tackle and lifting gear suitable to the loads; rigging the load safely and securely
- supervise the rigging crew
- ensure that the load is properly rigged
- ensure that signallers are capable of directing the crane and load, including use of the international hand signals where other forms of communication are not possible
- designate signallers and identify them to the operator
- ensure the safety of the rigging crew and other personnel affected by crane operations
- keep the public and all non-essential personnel clear of the crane during operation
- control the movements of all personnel in the area affected by the lift
- ensure all required precautions when the lift is near powerlines
- ensure that all personnel involved in the operation understand their jobs, responsibilities, and their role in the overall safety of each lift.

Basic Types and Configurations

The evolution of the mobile crane has led to many types and designs to satisfy both the general as well as the specific needs of construction and industrial operations. This manual is concerned with mobile cranes used for construction purposes as well as industrial applications.

The basic operational characteristics of all mobile cranes are essentially the same. They include:

- Adjustable boom lengths
- Adjustable boom angles
- Ability to lift and lower loads
- Ability to swing loads
- Ability to travel about the job site under their own power.

Within the broad category of mobile cranes there have evolved the following basic types and configurations:

- Boom Trucks
- Industrial Cranes
- Carrier-Mounted Lattice Boom Cranes
- Crawler-Mounted Lattice Boom Cranes
- Carrier-Mounted Telescopic Boom Cranes
- Crawler-Mounted Telescopic Boom Cranes
- Rough Terrain Cranes
- Mobile Tower Cranes
- Heavy Lift Mobile Cranes
- Spider Cranes
- Radial Boom Derricks.

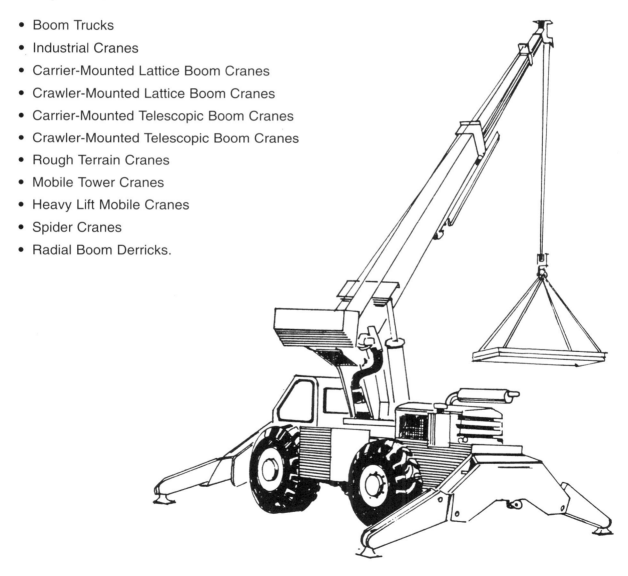

Boom Trucks

Unlike all other mobiles, boom trucks are mounted on carriers not designed solely for crane service. Instead, they are mounted on a commercial truck chassis that has been specially strengthened to accept the crane. They are, however, a type of mobile crane with respectable capacity and boom length.

There are two common configurations for this basic type of machine:
1. **Telescoping Boom**
2. **Articulating Crane**.

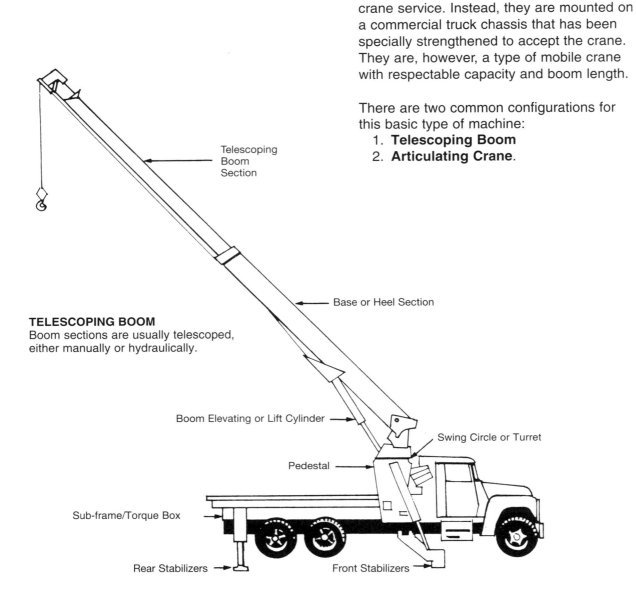

Telescoping Boom Section

Base or Heel Section

TELESCOPING BOOM
Boom sections are usually telescoped, either manually or hydraulically.

Boom Elevating or Lift Cylinder

Swing Circle or Turret

Pedestal

Sub-frame/Torque Box

Rear Stabilizers

Front Stabilizers

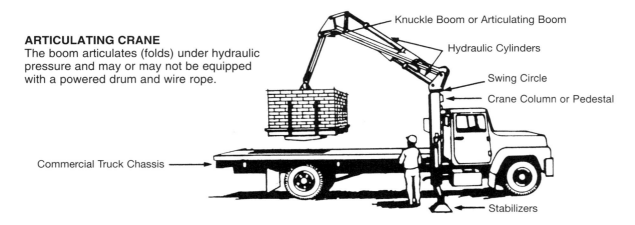

ARTICULATING CRANE
The boom articulates (folds) under hydraulic pressure and may or may not be equipped with a powered drum and wire rope.

Knuckle Boom or Articulating Boom

Hydraulic Cylinders

Swing Circle

Crane Column or Pedestal

Commercial Truck Chassis

Stabilizers

Industrial Cranes

These cranes are primarily intended for operation in industrial locations where working surfaces are significantly better than those found on most construction sites.

Although these cranes will not be analyzed specifically, their characteristics are basically identical to those of telescopic boom mobiles, which are covered in detail.

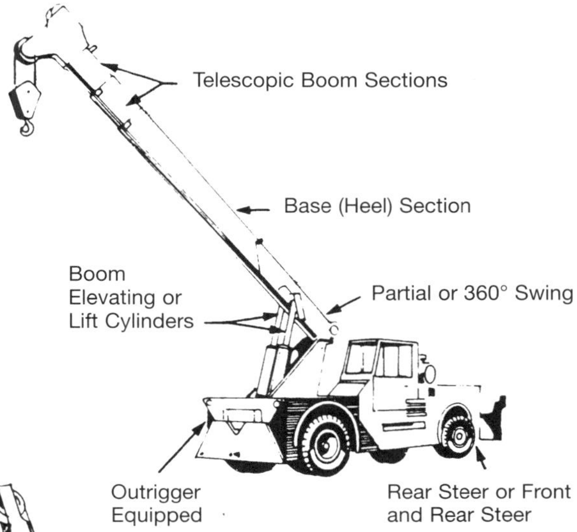

Telescopic Boom Sections

Base (Heel) Section

Boom Elevating or Lift Cylinders

Partial or 360° Swing

Outrigger Equipped

Rear Steer or Front and Rear Steer

PICK AND CARRY

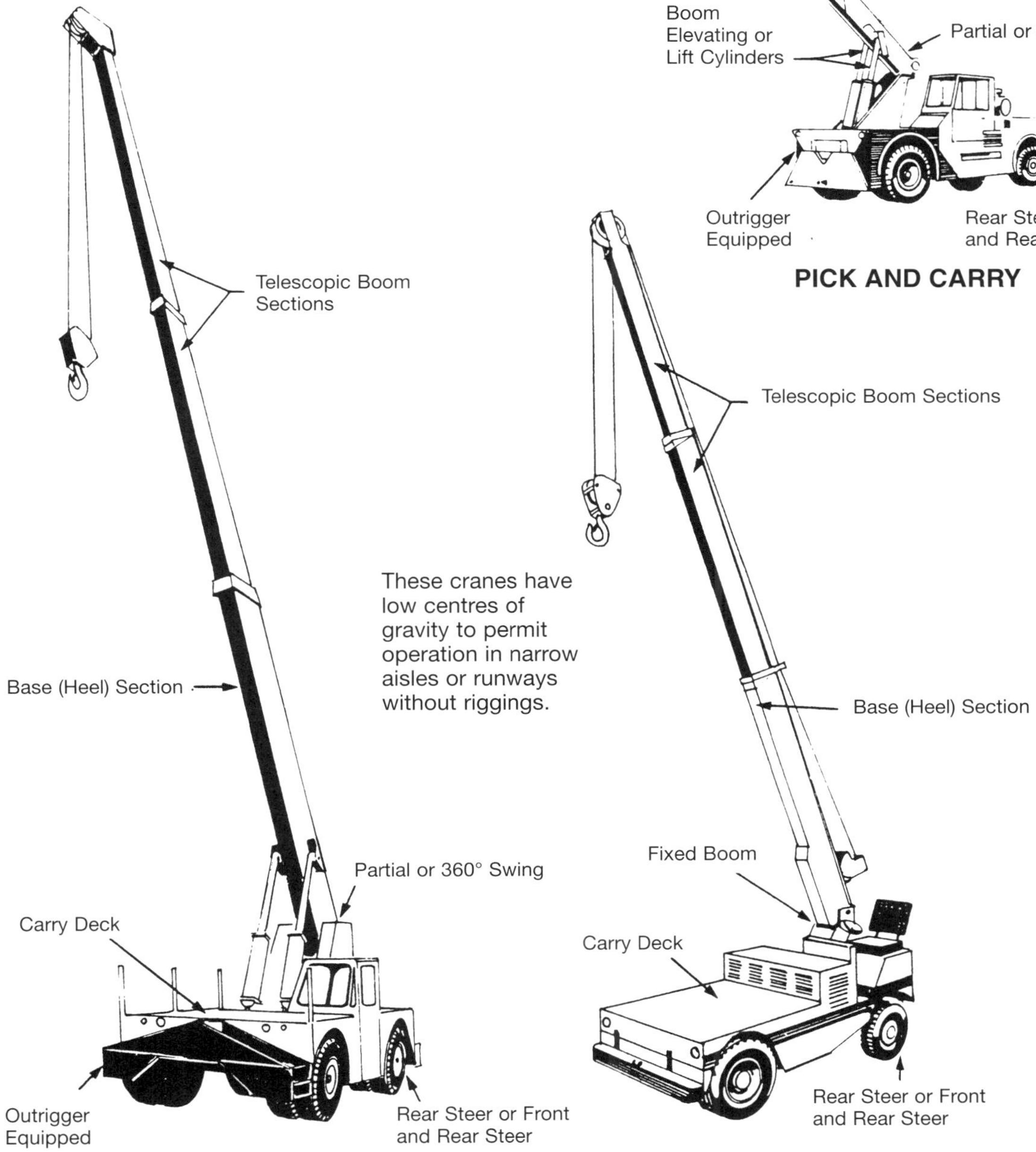

Telescopic Boom Sections

Telescopic Boom Sections

These cranes have low centres of gravity to permit operation in narrow aisles or runways without riggings.

Base (Heel) Section

Base (Heel) Section

Partial or 360° Swing

Fixed Boom

Carry Deck

Carry Deck

Outrigger Equipped

Rear Steer or Front and Rear Steer

Rear Steer or Front and Rear Steer

CARRY DECK – ROTATING BOOM   **CARRY DECK – FIXED BOOM**

Carrier-Mounted Lattice Boom Cranes

This "truck type" carrier must not be confused with the ordinary commercial truck chassis. It is specially designed for crane service and the heavy loads these cranes are required to withstand.

Carrier-mounted cranes are also commonly referred to as "Truck Cranes", "Conventional Cranes", "Friction Cranes", "Mobile Cranes", etc.

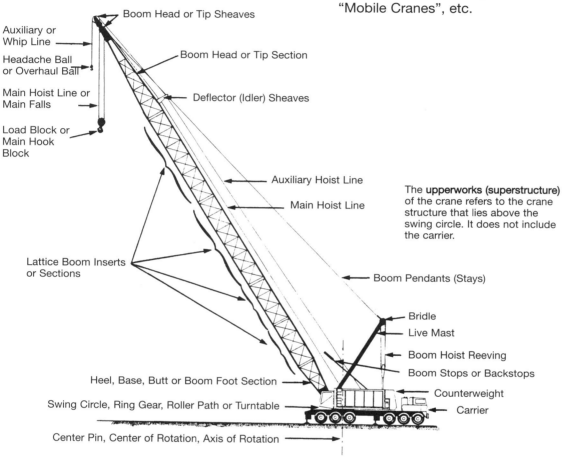

Boom Head or Tip Sheaves

Auxiliary or Whip Line

Headache Ball or Overhaul Ball

Boom Head or Tip Section

Main Hoist Line or Main Falls

Deflector (Idler) Sheaves

Load Block or Main Hook Block

Auxiliary Hoist Line

Main Hoist Line

The **upperworks (superstructure)** of the crane refers to the crane structure that lies above the swing circle. It does not include the carrier.

Lattice Boom Inserts or Sections

Boom Pendants (Stays)

Bridle

Live Mast

Boom Hoist Reeving

Boom Stops or Backstops

Heel, Base, Butt or Boom Foot Section

Counterweight

Swing Circle, Ring Gear, Roller Path or Turntable

Carrier

Center Pin, Center of Rotation, Axis of Rotation

Mid-Point (Intermediate) Suspension
Necessary when raising very long booms off the ground. They prevent the boom from sagging excessively.

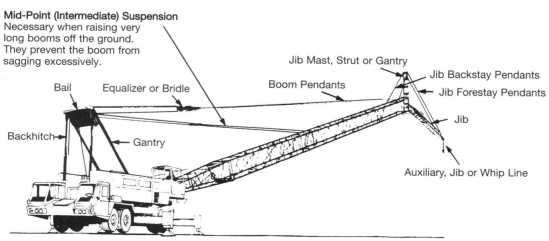

Jib Mast, Strut or Gantry

Jib Backstay Pendants

Boom Pendants

Jib Forestay Pendants

Bail

Equalizer or Bridle

Jib

Backhitch

Gantry

Auxiliary, Jib or Whip Line

Carrier-Mounted Lattice Boom Cranes (continued)

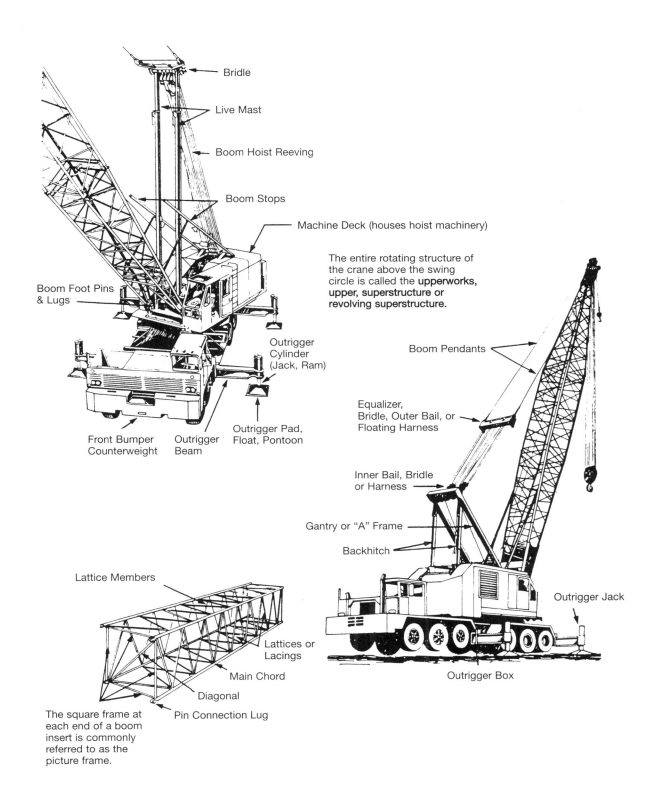

Bridle

Live Mast

Boom Hoist Reeving

Boom Stops

Machine Deck (houses hoist machinery)

Boom Foot Pins & Lugs

The entire rotating structure of the crane above the swing circle is called the **upperworks, upper, superstructure or revolving superstructure.**

Outrigger Cylinder (Jack, Ram)

Boom Pendants

Equalizer, Bridle, Outer Bail, or Floating Harness

Inner Bail, Bridle or Harness

Gantry or "A" Frame

Backhitch

Front Bumper Counterweight

Outrigger Beam

Outrigger Pad, Float, Pontoon

Outrigger Jack

Outrigger Box

Lattice Members

Lattices or Lacings

Main Chord

Diagonal

Pin Connection Lug

The square frame at each end of a boom insert is commonly referred to as the picture frame.

Crawler-Mounted Lattice Boom Cranes

Except for their base and method of load rating, the upperworks of these machines are identical to the carrier-mounted units.

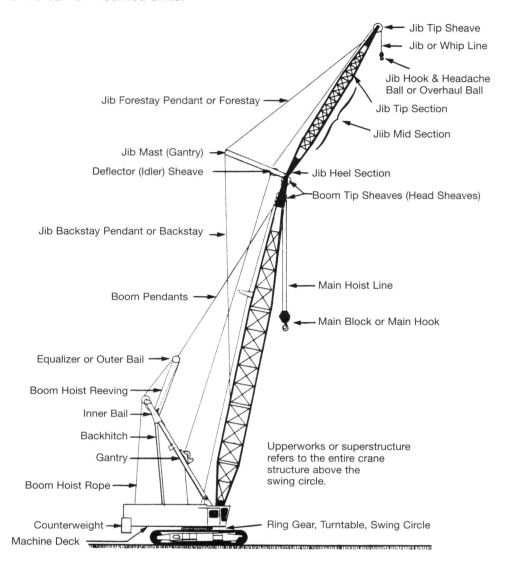

Jib Tip Sheave

Jib or Whip Line

Jib Hook & Headache Ball or Overhaul Ball

Jib Tip Section

Jiib Mid Section

Jib Forestay Pendant or Forestay

Jib Mast (Gantry)

Deflector (Idler) Sheave

Jib Heel Section

Boom Tip Sheaves (Head Sheaves)

Jib Backstay Pendant or Backstay

Main Hoist Line

Boom Pendants

Main Block or Main Hook

Equalizer or Outer Bail

Boom Hoist Reeving

Inner Bail

Backhitch

Gantry

Upperworks or superstructure refers to the entire crane structure above the swing circle.

Boom Hoist Rope

Counterweight

Ring Gear, Turntable, Swing Circle

Machine Deck

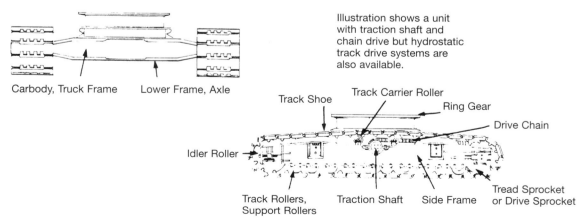

Carbody, Truck Frame   Lower Frame, Axle

Illustration shows a unit with traction shaft and chain drive but hydrostatic track drive systems are also available.

Track Shoe

Track Carrier Roller

Ring Gear

Drive Chain

Idler Roller

Track Rollers, Support Rollers

Traction Shaft

Side Frame

Tread Sprocket or Drive Sprocket

Carrier-Mounted Telescopic Boom Cranes

These machines are also mounted on specially designed carriers. They can be equipped with a variety of jibs and boom extensions which can be stowed on or under the heel section of the main boom.

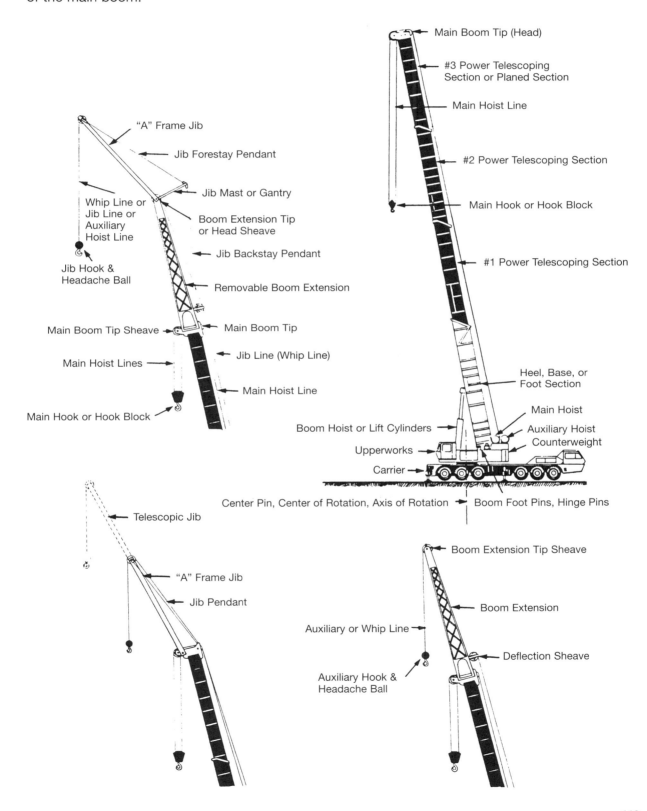

"A" Frame Jib

Jib Forestay Pendant

Jib Mast or Gantry

Whip Line or Jib Line or Auxiliary Hoist Line

Boom Extension Tip or Head Sheave

Jib Backstay Pendant

Jib Hook & Headache Ball

Removable Boom Extension

Main Boom Tip Sheave

Main Boom Tip

Main Hoist Lines

Jib Line (Whip Line)

Main Hoist Line

Main Hook or Hook Block

Main Boom Tip (Head)

#3 Power Telescoping Section or Planed Section

Main Hoist Line

#2 Power Telescoping Section

Main Hook or Hook Block

#1 Power Telescoping Section

Heel, Base, or Foot Section

Main Hoist

Auxiliary Hoist

Counterweight

Boom Hoist or Lift Cylinders

Upperworks

Carrier

Center Pin, Center of Rotation, Axis of Rotation

Boom Foot Pins, Hinge Pins

Telescopic Jib

"A" Frame Jib

Jib Pendant

Boom Extension Tip Sheave

Boom Extension

Auxiliary or Whip Line

Deflection Sheave

Auxiliary Hook & Headache Ball

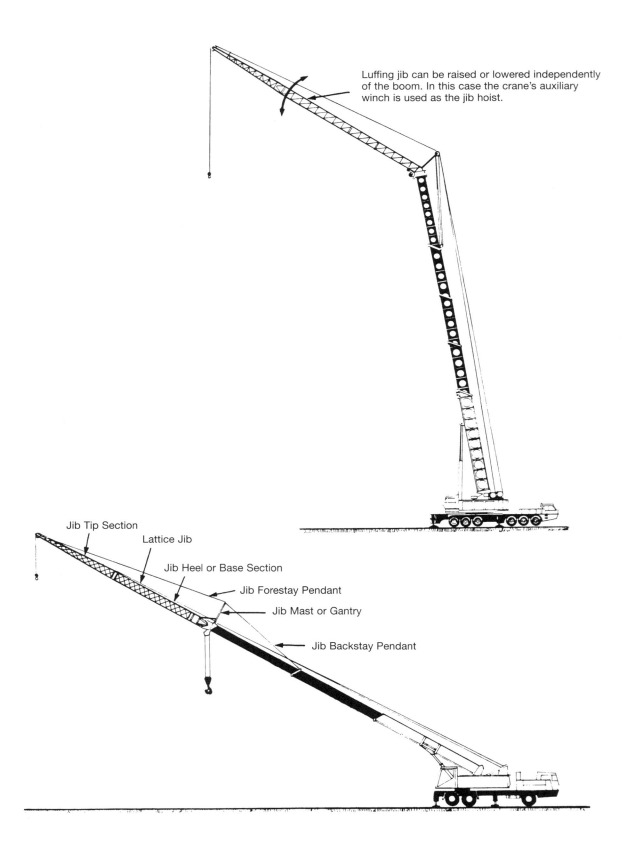

Luffing jib can be raised or lowered independently of the boom. In this case the crane's auxiliary winch is used as the jib hoist.

Jib Tip Section

Lattice Jib

Jib Heel or Base Section

Jib Forestay Pendant

Jib Mast or Gantry

Jib Backstay Pendant

Carrier-Mounted Telescopic Boom Cranes (continued)

Carrier-mounted telescopic boom cranes are subdivided by the type of head section (boom tip section) they are equipped with.

FULL POWER BOOMS

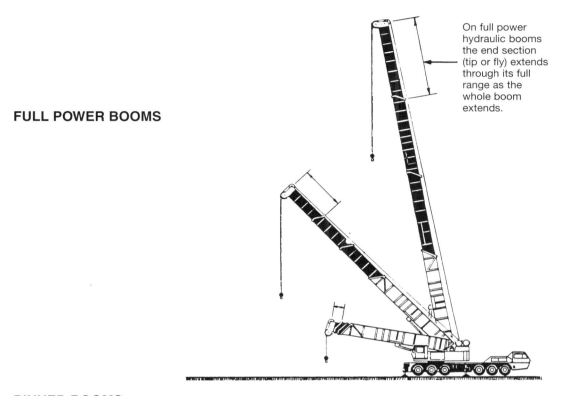

On full power hydraulic booms the end section (tip or fly) extends through its full range as the whole boom extends.

PINNED BOOMS

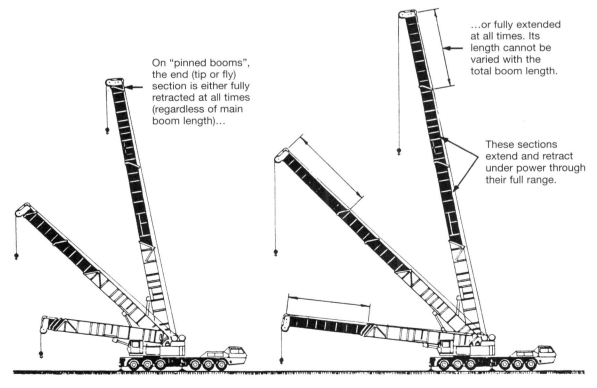

On "pinned booms", the end (tip or fly) section is either fully retracted at all times (regardless of main boom length)...

...or fully extended at all times. Its length cannot be varied with the total boom length.

These sections extend and retract under power through their full range.

Crawler-Mounted Telescopic Boom Cranes

The upperworks of these cranes are identical to the carrier-mounted telescopic boom units. Their bases and the method used to load rate them differ, however.

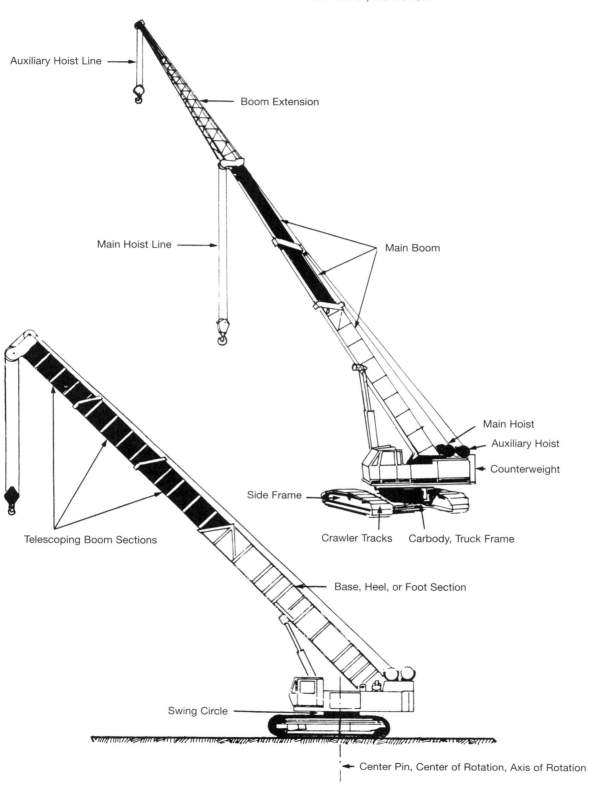

Auxiliary Hoist Line

Boom Extension

Main Hoist Line

Main Boom

Main Hoist

Auxiliary Hoist

Counterweight

Side Frame

Crawler Tracks

Carbody, Truck Frame

Telescoping Boom Sections

Base, Heel, or Foot Section

Swing Circle

Center Pin, Center of Rotation, Axis of Rotation

Rough Terrain Cranes

The rough terrain crane's oversized tires facilitate movement across the rough terrain of construction sites and other broken ground. Their short wheel base and crab-steering improve maneuverability. In "pick and carry" operations on rough terrain, however, they are still subject to the same operating restrictions that apply to other cranes.

Like carrier-mounted telescopic boom cranes, rough terrain units are available with either full power booms or pinned booms and the same types of jibs and boom extensions. There are two basic configurations.

FIXED CAB

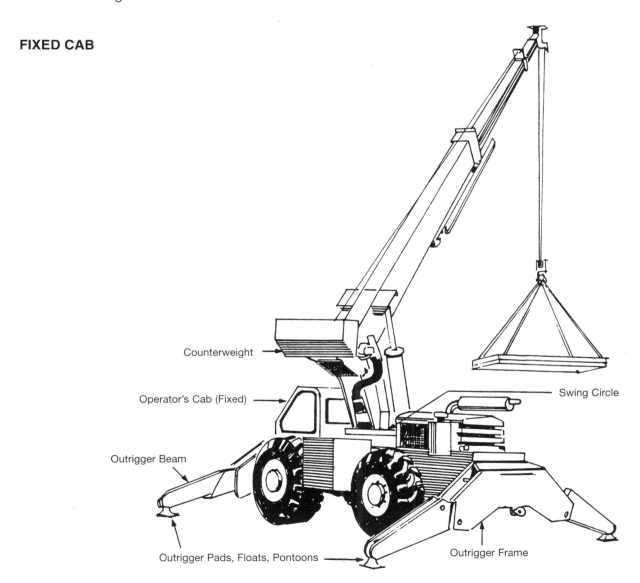

Counterweight

Operator's Cab (Fixed)

Swing Circle

Outrigger Beam

Outrigger Pads, Floats, Pontoons

Outrigger Frame

Rough Terrain Cranes (continued)

ROTATING CAB

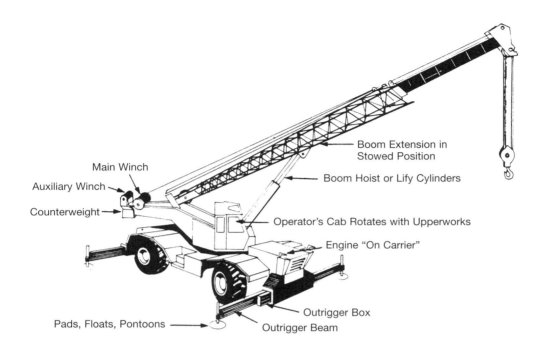

Main Winch

Auxiliary Winch

Counterweight

Boom Extension in Stowed Position

Boom Hoist or Lify Cylinders

Operator's Cab Rotates with Upperworks

Engine "On Carrier"

Outrigger Box

Pads, Floats, Pontoons

Outrigger Beam

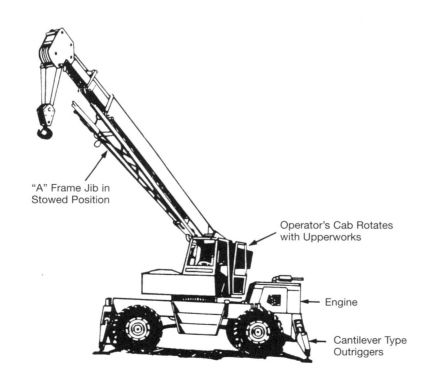

"A" Frame Jib in Stowed Position

Operator's Cab Rotates with Upperworks

Engine

Cantilever Type Outriggers

Rough Terrain Cranes (continued)

Like the carrier-mounted telescopic boom cranes, rough terrain cranes can be equipped with either full power booms or pinned booms as well as with a variety of jibs and boom extensions which can also be stowed on or under the heel section of the main boom.

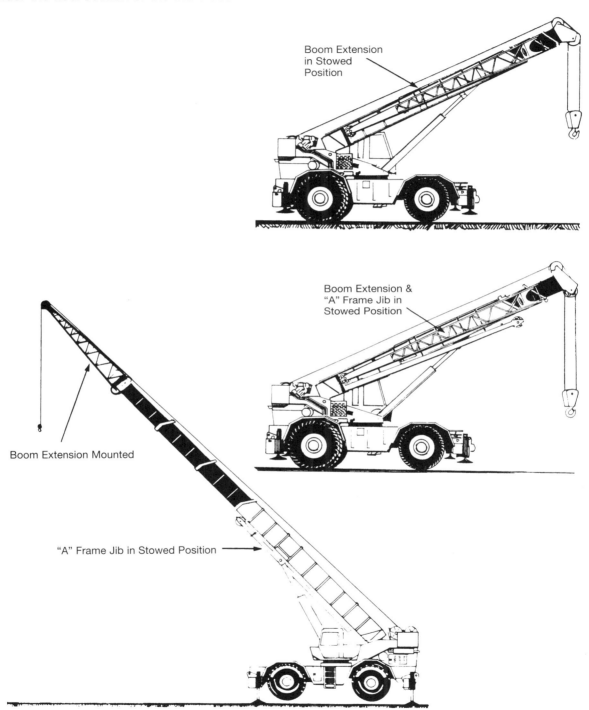

Boom Extension in Stowed Position

Boom Extension & "A" Frame Jib in Stowed Position

Boom Extension Mounted

"A" Frame Jib in Stowed Position

Heavy Lift Mobile Cranes

These cranes combine the best features of derricks and lattice boom mobile cranes. Typically they use very large extended counterweights, masts and often roller rings that move the boom's fulcrum and the crane's tipping axis further away from the center of gravity.

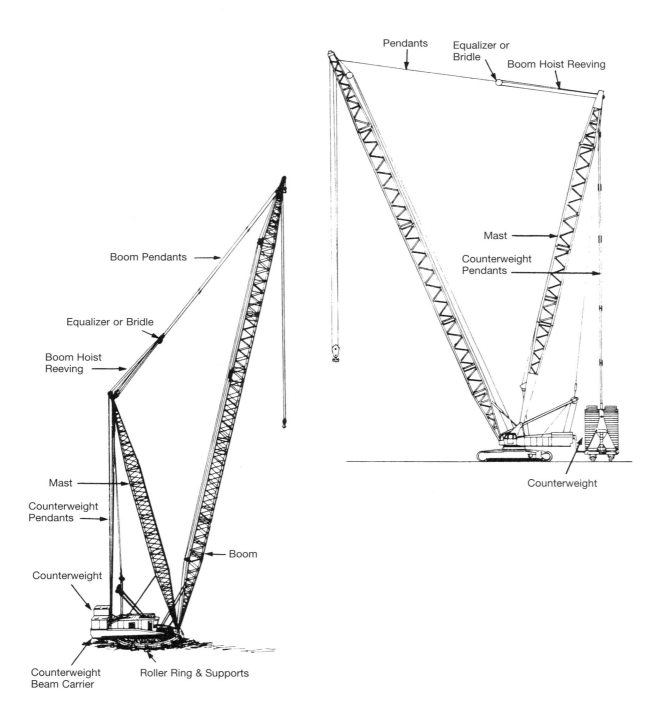

Boom Pendants

Equalizer or Bridle

Boom Hoist Reeving

Mast

Counterweight Pendants

Counterweight

Counterweight Beam Carrier

Roller Ring & Supports

Boom

Pendants

Equalizer or Bridle

Boom Hoist Reeving

Mast

Counterweight Pendants

Counterweight

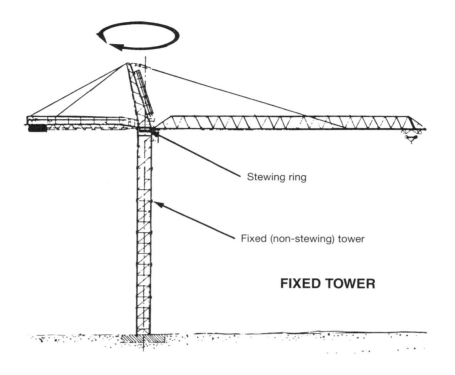

Stewing ring

Fixed (non-stewing) tower

FIXED TOWER

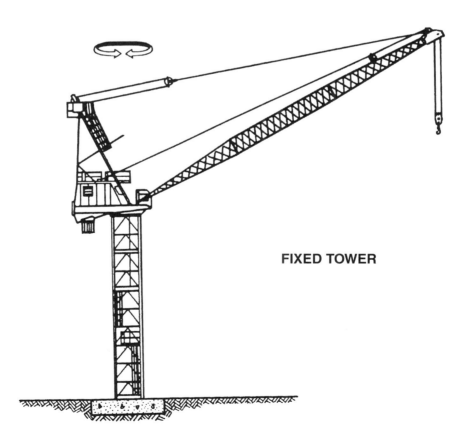

FIXED TOWER

Hazards in Crane Operating Areas

Over 50% of all mobile crane accidents are the result of mistakes made when the crane was being set up.

All of these accidents can be prevented by following the manufacturer's recommendations for assembly and dismantling, by using the correct components, and by observing the precautions outlined in this section.

Remember: Improvising or taking shortcuts in assembly and setup can be fatal.

Use the checklist on the next page for reviewing the factors to consider in planning for crane and hoisting operations.

PRE-JOB CHECKLIST

Whoever requires that a crane be used-project engineer, site superintendent, foreperson, building owner, contractor, architect, or consultant – is as responsible for its safe operation as the operator.

If a working area has not been adequately prepared for the crane, the operation will be unsafe, regardless of machine capacity or operator skill. Consider the following factors.

- Can the machine get onto the site? Is the access road adequately graded and compacted? Is the access ramp too steep?

- Will the machine have to travel over buried pipes, sewers, mains, etc., that might be crushed?

- Is there room for the crane to maneuver in its designated position on site? Is there room to erect or extend the boom? Can trucks hauling boom sections get into position and be unloaded safely? Is there enough room and timber blocking to store boom sections properly?

- Will an area be designated and roped off for use by the erection crew? Will it be large enough for components to be stacked, handled, and assembled without endangering other site personnel?

- Has the crane's position been identified for every lift? What will the maximum operating radius be? Will there be at least two feet of clearance between the counterweight and nearest object? What obstacles or other hazards might be posed by existing buildings or structures?

- Are operating areas graded, compacted, and levelled? Are they away from shoring locations, excavations, slopes, trenches, embankments, etc., which could subside under machine weight and vibration? Are operating areas over cellars, buried pipes, mains, etc., that may collapse?

- Will clearance and visibility be problems where other cranes, hoists, or equipment will be operating? Will operators have a clear view of other equipment to avoid collisions and keep hoisting ropes and loads from fouling? Will operators be provided with direct communication to warn one another of impending danger? Will the overall lifting program be laid out, controlled, and prioritized by one person in contact with all operators and each rigging crew?

- Will crane operating areas be away from public traffic and access? Will signallers and warning signs be provided when crane operations may overlap with public areas? Has police cooperation been arranged to provide traffic and pedestrian control?

- Have operators been warned and have provisions been made to keep cranes from working within a boom's length of powerlines without

  a) shutting off power

  b) having the powerlines insulated, or

  c) providing signallers to warn the operator when any part of the crane or load nears the limits of approach specified by the *Regulations for Construction Projects*?

Voltage Rating of Powerline	Minimum Distance
750 to 150,000 volts	3 metres (10')
150,001 to 250,000 volts	4.5 metres (15')
over 250,000 volts	6 metres (20')

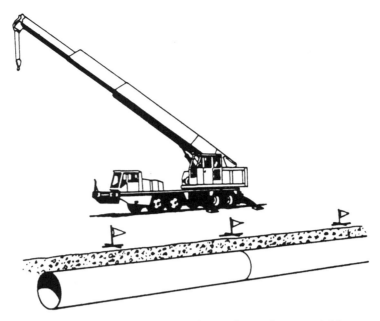

Mark the location of all underground services that could be crushed by the weight of the crane.

SWING

Fence or barricade areas in which personnel could be trapped and crushed.

Danger Areas

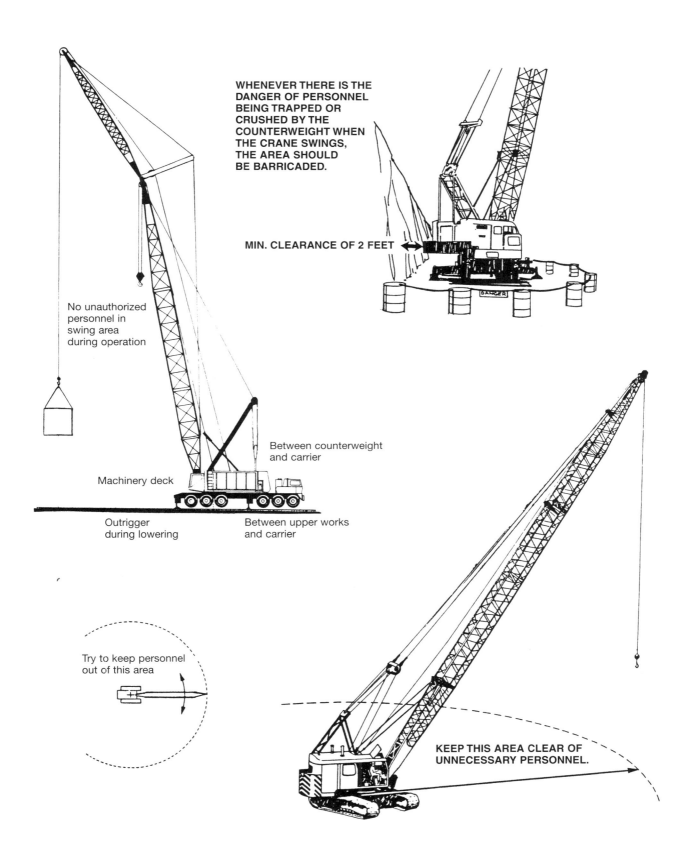

WHENEVER THERE IS THE DANGER OF PERSONNEL BEING TRAPPED OR CRUSHED BY THE COUNTERWEIGHT WHEN THE CRANE SWINGS, THE AREA SHOULD BE BARRICADED.

MIN. CLEARANCE OF 2 FEET

No unauthorized personnel in swing area during operation

Between counterweight and carrier

Machinery deck

Outrigger during lowering

Between upper works and carrier

Try to keep personnel out of this area

KEEP THIS AREA CLEAR OF UNNECESSARY PERSONNEL.

Working Near Powerlines

High voltage electrocution is the largest single cause of fatalities associated with cranes. All can be prevented. The power company or utility may consider (if given advance notification) shutting down the line temporarily or moving the line. If it is not possible to have the line moved or the power shut off the following procedures should be **enforced by the project supervisor and strictly followed by all operators.**

1. **KEEP YOUR DISTANCE.** Surrounding every live powerline is an area where an electric arc is capable of jumping from the powerline to a conductor of electricity. So you must keep all of your equipment and its load at least the **minimum permitted distance** away from the powerline (see page 6 for distances). If there is a chance for any part of the hoisting operation to encroach on that distance, protective measures must be taken to prevent this encroachment. You must take these measures unless you have controlled the hazard by de-energizing or moving the lines, or by re-routing the electricity around the work.

Note: The only exception to these requirements occurs under both of these conditions:
- the powerline cannot be de-energized or moved, or the electricity re-routed, **and**
- *under the authority of the owner of the electrical conductor,* protective devices and equipment are installed and written procedures are implemented that are adequate to protect equipment operators from electrical shock and burn.

This absolute limit of approach varies according to local, provincial, state and federal laws or crane manufacturer's recommendations, but is generally as shown:

see page 6 for distances

OPERATORS
Before setting up to operate, look up. If there are powerlines, advise your supervisor. The presence of overhead powerlines may require a written work procedure.

SITE SUPERVISION
Where a crane, hoist line, or load can cross into the minimum distance to an overhead powerline, the constructor must have written procedures in place to prevent the crane, hoistline, or load from encroaching on the minimum distance.

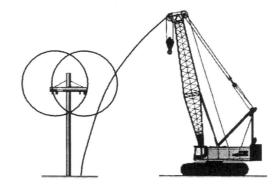

The crane boom could reach within the minimum distance.

PRE-JOB PLANNING
The time to take care of powerline problems is during pre-job planning after the first site survey is made by a contractor. Take care of the problem prior to the crane's arrival to avoid job delays and prevent accidents.

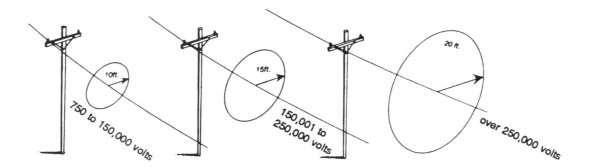

10ft. — 750 to 150,000 volts

15ft. — 150,001 to 250,000 volts

20 ft. — over 250,000 volts

2. Treat all powerlines as live until reliable information assures you that the lines are de-energized.

Working near Powerlines (continued)

3. Identify the voltage of the service by checking markings on the utility pole and calling the utility. When equipment or its load can encroach on the minimum permitted distance from a powerline, the constructor must have written procedures in place to prevent the equipment or its load from encroaching on the minimum distance.

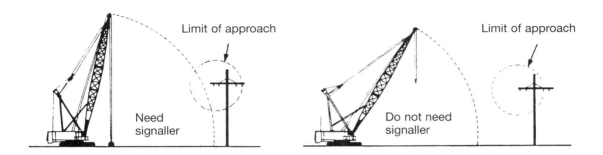

Limit of approach

Need signaller

Limit of approach

Do not need signaller

4. Have powerlines moved, insulated, de-energized, or follow the precautions in the Construction Regulation. Insulating or "rubberizing" powerlines offers some protection in case of brush contact in some circumstances. Your local utility may provide this service.

5. Place enough warning devices (such as signs) near the hazard so that the equipment operator can always see at least one of them. The operator must be able to see them under all possible environmental conditions (e.g., night, rain, fog). Signs must be specific about the hazard. They should state, for example, *"Danger! Electrical powerlines overhead."* IHSA recommends that you include the voltage on the sign.

6. The operator's station (e.g., driver's cab) must have a sign (such as a sticker) warning of the hazard. The machine may come with a warning sticker in the cab. Make sure it's still legible.

7. A competent worker must be designated as a signaller to warn the operator when any part of the equipment, load, or hoist line approaches the minimum permitted distance to a powerline. The signaler must be in full view of the operator and have a clear view of both the equipment and the electrical conductor.

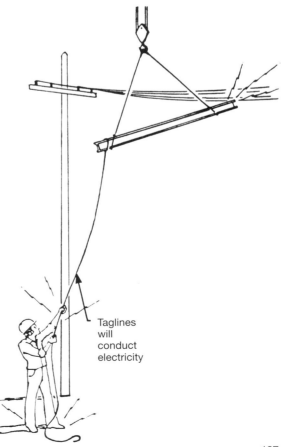

Taglines will conduct electricity

Working near Powerlines (continued)

8. Avoid using tag lines. Unless it is necessary to prevent the load from spinning into the minimum distance to a powerline, the tag line itself can be a hazard because it can swing into the minimum distance.

   Note: All ropes are capable of conducting electricity, but dry polypropylene has better insulating properties than most commercially-available ropes.

9. Slow down the operating cycle of the machine by reducing hoisting, booming, swinging, and travel speeds.

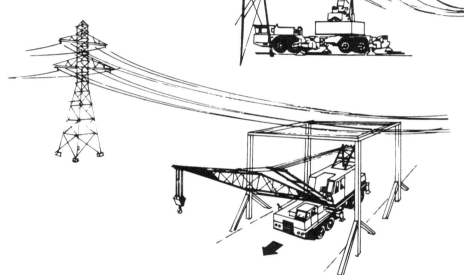

Accidental contact from powerline swaying in the wind

10. Exercise caution when working near overhead lines having long spans as they tend to swing laterally in the wind and accidental contact could occur.

11. Exercise caution when travelling the crane as uneven ground can cause the boom to weave or bob into the lines.

12. Ensure that whenever cranes must repeatedly travel beneath powerlines a route is plainly marked and "rider poles" are erected on each side of the crossing approach to ensure that the crane structure is lowered to a safe height.

IF YOU MAKE ELECTRICAL CONTACT WITH A POWERLINE

- **Stay on the equipment.** Don't touch the equipment and the ground at the same time. In fact, touching anything in contact with the ground can be fatal. If a new hazard develops that could be life-threatening, such as a fire, use the "bailout procedure" (next page).

- **Keep others away.** No one else should touch the equipment or its load – including buckets, outriggers, load lines, or any other part of the machine. Beware of time-delayed relays: Even after electrical contact trips the breakers, relays may still try to restore power. They may come on automatically two or three times.

- **Break contact.** If possible – while remaining inside the machine – the operator should try to break contact by moving the equipment clear of the wires. This may be impossible if contact has welded conductors to the equipment.

- **Call the local utility.** Get someone to call the local electrical utility for help. Stay on the equipment until the utility shuts down the line and confirms that the power is off.

- **Report the contact.** Report every incident of electrical contact to the local electrical utility – they'll check for damage that could cause the line to fail later.

  When the powerline is rated at 750 volts or more:

  1. report the contact to the inspection department of the Electrical Safety Authority within 48 hours.

  2. provide notice in writing to the Ministry of Labour and to the joint health and safety committee, health and safety representative, and trade union.

- **Inspect the crane.** The crane must undergo a complete inspection for possible damage caused by electrical contact. The electric cur-rent could take several paths through the crane, damaging bearings, electronic controls, valves, and the crane's cable. Wire rope should be replaced. Damage to the wire rope – such as welding, melting, or pitting – may not be visible.

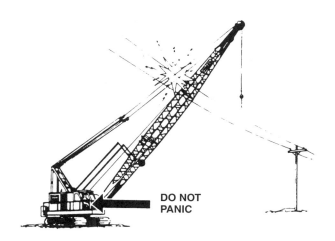

DO NOT PANIC

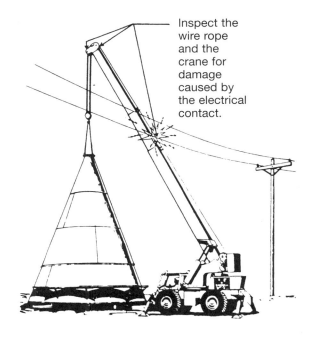

Inspect the wire rope and the crane for damage caused by the electrical contact.

Working near Powerlines (continued)

BAILOUT PROCEDURE

If the operator decides to leave the machine, he must *jump* clear. He must never step down allowing part of his body to be in contact with the ground while any other part is touching the machine.

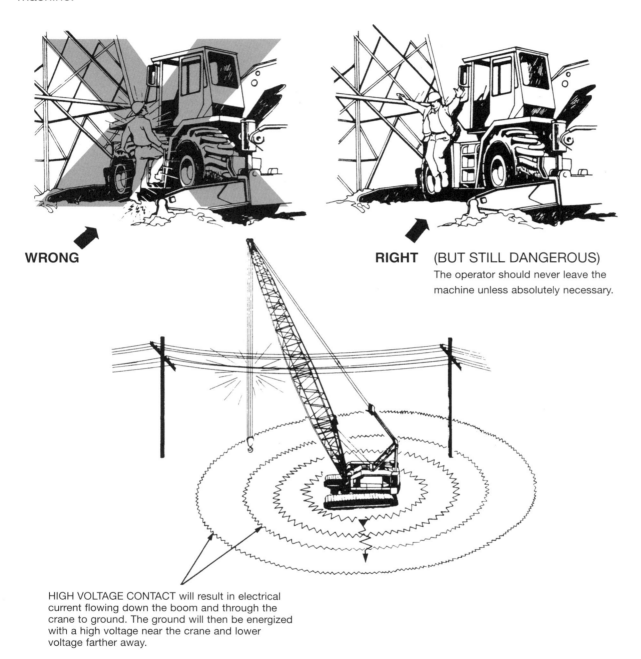

WRONG

RIGHT (BUT STILL DANGEROUS)
The operator should never leave the machine unless absolutely necessary.

HIGH VOLTAGE CONTACT will result in electrical current flowing down the boom and through the crane to ground. The ground will then be energized with a high voltage near the crane and lower voltage farther away.

Because of the hazardous voltage differential in the ground, the operator should jump with his feet together, maintain balance and shuffle voltage slowly across the affected area. Do not take large steps because it is possible for one foot to be in a high voltage area, and the other to be in a lower voltage area. The difference between the two can kill.

Working Near Transmitters

When operating near radio, TV or microwave transmitters the crane boom and load can become electrically charged. The boom acts like an antenna and becomes "hot". The charge is not electrically dangerous when compared with the effect of contacting electricity but it can cause burns to personnel handling loads. The greatest danger to personnel exists when they "jump" from the effect of this shock and fall or trip.

Grounding the crane will not likely have any effect. The only real solution is to insert a synthetic web sling between the crane's load block and the load. This will isolate the riggers from the crane and protect them from burns. The crane operator will not be affected when in the machine but should wear rubber gloves when getting on and off the crane.

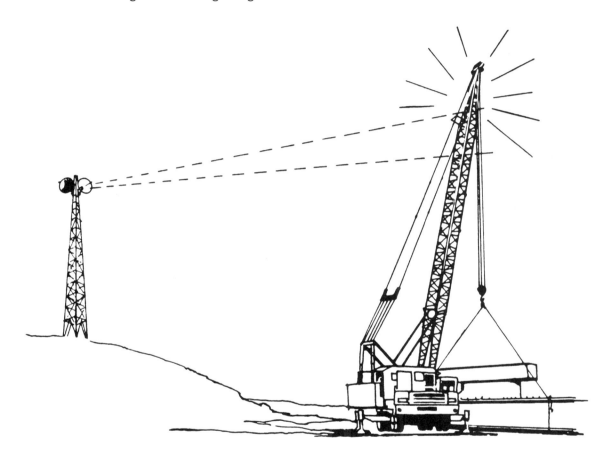

Factors Affecting Crane Capacity

Capacities and other information included in the load charts for cranes are based on almost perfect conditions seldom achieved under actual operation.

It is vital to know not only how to determine capacity correctly from the chart but also to recognize the factors that can reduce a crane's capacity below the chart ratings.

These factors, described on the following pages, include:

- poor machine condition
- variations in boom angle
- variations in load radius
- errors in boom angle indicators during critical lifts
- quadrants of operation
- sweep area
- tires not clear of the ground
- division of sweep area into quadrants
- improper use of outriggers
- soft footing
- crane not level
- sideloading
- increase in load radius
- rapid swing rate
- impact loading
- rapid acceleration or deceleration of load
- duty cycle operations
- high wind speeds.

The information concludes with an illustration of proper setup.

Poor Machine Condition

Load chart ratings apply only to cranes maintained in condition as good as new and as stipulated by the manufacturer. The boom is one of the more critical elements of the crane and *must* be in perfect condition at all times.

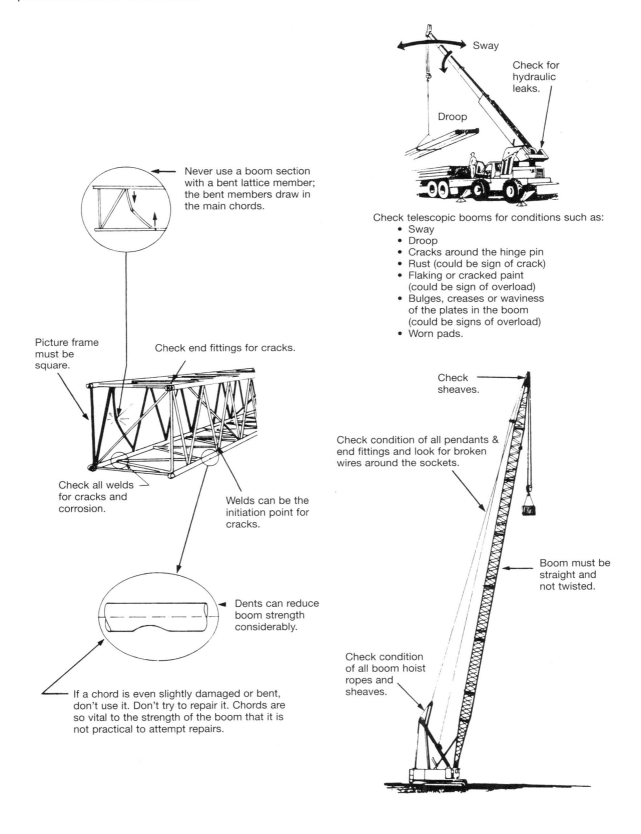

Never use a boom section with a bent lattice member; the bent members draw in the main chords.

Picture frame must be square.

Check end fittings for cracks.

Check all welds for cracks and corrosion.

Welds can be the initiation point for cracks.

Dents can reduce boom strength considerably.

If a chord is even slightly damaged or bent, don't use it. Don't try to repair it. Chords are so vital to the strength of the boom that it is not practical to attempt repairs.

Sway

Check for hydraulic leaks.

Droop

Check telescopic booms for conditions such as:
• Sway
• Droop
• Cracks around the hinge pin
• Rust (could be sign of crack)
• Flaking or cracked paint (could be sign of overload)
• Bulges, creases or waviness of the plates in the boom (could be signs of overload)
• Worn pads.

Check sheaves.

Check condition of all pendants & end fittings and look for broken wires around the sockets.

Boom must be straight and not twisted.

Check condition of all boom hoist ropes and sheaves.

Boom Angle

The capacities listed in the load chart are also based on and vary with the boom angle of the machine.

On telescopic boom cranes the boom angle is the angle between the base (bottom) of the heel section of the main boom and the horizontal *while the boom is under load.*

Because of boom and machine deflection (and pendant stretch on lattice booms) expect the boom angle to lower somewhat from its unloaded condition once a load is applied. Expect even larger boom angle reductions when the crane is "on rubber" because of tire deflection.

Load Radius

The capacities listed in the load chart also depend on and vary with the crane's load radius. The load radius is the horizontal distance measured from the center of rotation of the crane (center pin) to the load hook (center of gravity of the load) *while* the boom is loaded.

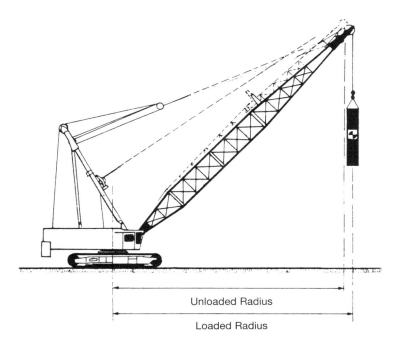

Unloaded Radius

Loaded Radius

Because of boom and machine deflection and pendant stretch, expect the load radius to increase when the load is lifted off the ground. Expect even larger increases in radius when the crane is "on rubber" because of tire deflection.

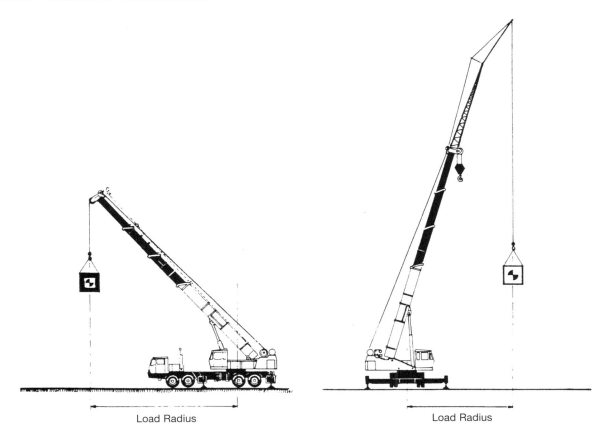

Load Radius

Load Radius

Boom Angle Indicators and Critical Lifts

Boom angle indicators are required on all mobile cranes but they must not be relied on for accuracy during critical lifts because:

- They can give as much as a 2° reading error in boom angle which can substantially affect the gross capacity reading on the load chart.
- The indicators are mounted on the base section of the boom and may not register the deflection of the extended sections under heavy load particularly if the wear pads are worn excessively. Consequently the boom angle may actually be lower than the indicator reads.

For these reasons, using boom angle indicator readings during critical lifts can be misleading. Rely on load radius (where possible) or if the boom angle must be used (for example when lifting from a jib) assume the correct reading to be *lower* than what the indicator actually says.

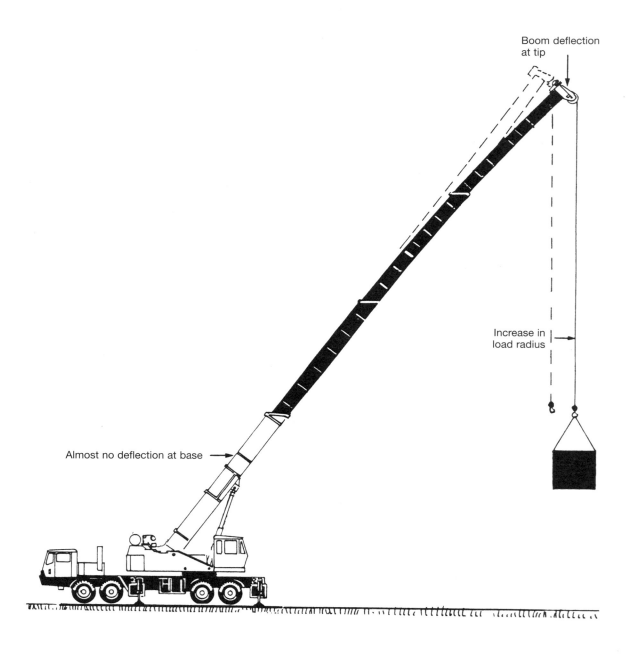

Boom deflection at tip

Increase in load radius

Almost no deflection at base

Importance of Quadrants

The leverage and capacity of a crane change during rotation of the upperworks. Leverage and capacity are also affected by the location of the tipping axis. For these reasons the crane's stability can change during operation.

To provide uniform stability, regardless of the position of the upperworks relative to the carrier, the crane's capacity is adjusted by the manufacturer according to the quadrant of operation.

These capacity changes are identified in the load chart by the quadrant of operation.

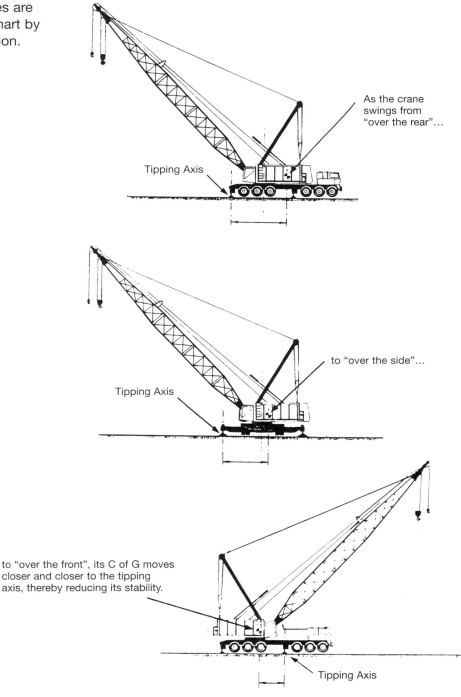

As the crane swings from "over the rear"...

Tipping Axis

to "over the side"...

Tipping Axis

to "over the front", its C of G moves closer and closer to the tipping axis, thereby reducing its stability.

Tipping Axis

Sweep Area

The sweep area is the total area that the crane boom can swing over.

The sweep area is divided into operating areas called quadrants of operation. The crane's capacity is then based on the quadrants.

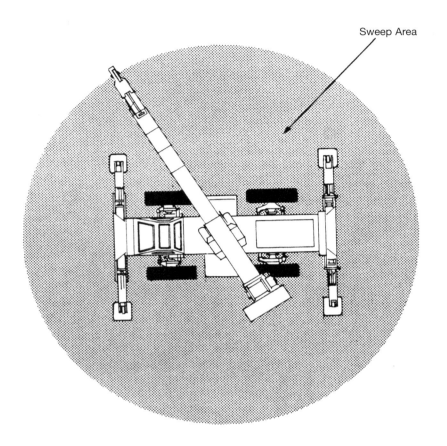

Sweep Area

Division of Sweep Area into Quadrants

The crane is said to be in a particular quadrant of operation when the load hook is located over that portion of the sweep area.

Caution: Not every make and model of crane can be operated in all of these quadrants. The diagrams are for reference only. Consult load charts to determine quadrants of operation for particular makes and models.

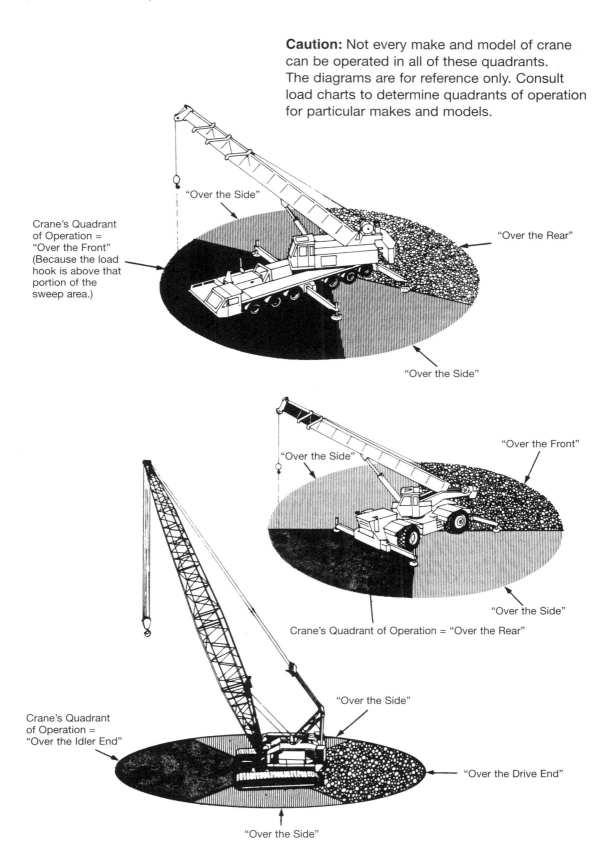

"Over the Side"

Crane's Quadrant of Operation = "Over the Front" (Because the load hook is above that portion of the sweep area.)

"Over the Rear"

"Over the Side"

"Over the Side"

"Over the Front"

"Over the Side"

Crane's Quadrant of Operation = "Over the Rear"

"Over the Side"

Crane's Quadrant of Operation = "Over the Idler End"

"Over the Drive End"

"Over the Side"

Improper Use of Outriggers

The load chart ratings of carrier-mounted and rough terrain mobile cranes apply to three base configurations:

- "On Outriggers"
- "On Tires"
- Partially Extended Outriggers

"On Outriggers"

Full chart ratings apply only when:

- all outrigger beams are fully extended, and
- all tires are clear of the ground.

Partially Extended Outriggers

In special circumstances a crane may be operated on outriggers that are not fully extended. In this situation the crane must be equipped with load charts coinciding with this partial extension of the outriggers and there must be a method of measuring the outrigger extension.

CRANE HAS "ON OUTRIGGERS" RATING

"ON TIRES" RATING
Crane does not have "on outriggers" rating because rear outriggers are not extended and set. This machine's capacity is limited to the "on tires" load chart.

Outriggers not extended and set.

Improper Use of Outriggers (continued)

"ON TIRES" RATING
Full "on outrigger" ratings do not apply because
the carrier wheels are touching the ground.

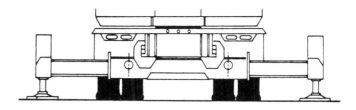

PARTIALLY EXTENDED OUTRIGGERS
Load charts must be supplied for this partial
extension. Otherwise use "On Tires" rating.

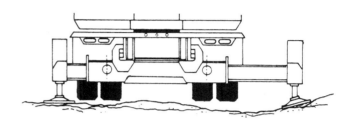

"ON OUTRIGGER" RATING
Full "on outrigger" ratings apply because
• all beams are fully extended
• all tires are clear of the ground.

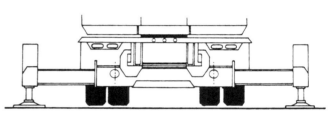

Tires should be just clear of the ground to keep ram length
as short as possible and thus minimize rocking action.

"On Tires"

Full chart ratings apply only when:

• tires are per manufacturer's specifications

• tires are in good condition

• specified tire pressure is maintained, and

• crane speed does not exceed manufacturer's
  specifications.

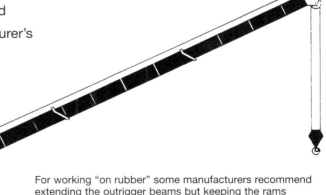

For working "on rubber" some manufacturers recommend
extending the outrigger beams but keeping the rams
partially retracted so that the floats are just clear of the
ground.

Soft Footing

Load chart ratings apply only when the ground conditions are firm enough to support the crane *and keep it level during the lift.* If the ground is soft or unstable, the tires, crawlers or outriggers will sink or subside causing loss of capacity. In almost all cases, heavy duty blocking having large bearing areas will be necessary to prevent sinking and provide a solid base for the crane.

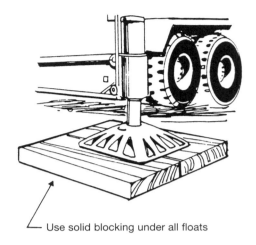

Use solid blocking under all floats

Poor Float Support

Poor Float Support

Poor Float Support

On soft ground or on backfilled material, timber or steel mats must be used to prevent the crane from sinking or setting.

Crane Not Level

All load chart ratings are based on the machine being perfectly level in all directions. This applies to cranes "on crawlers", "on tires", "on outriggers" and when travelling with load.

One of the most severe effects of being out-of-level is that side loads develop in the boom. Because of side loads all mobile cranes lose capacity *rapidly* as the degree of out-of-level increases.

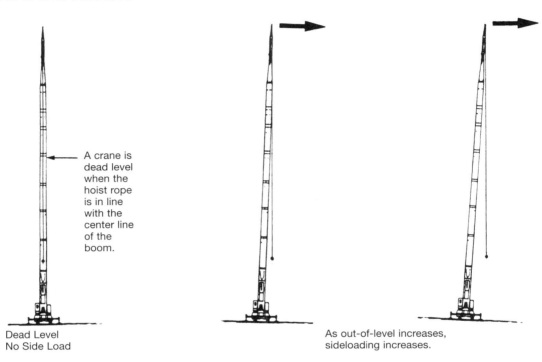

A crane is dead level when the hoist rope is in line with the center line of the boom.

Dead Level
No Side Load

As out-of-level increases, sideloading increases.

Being level is critical to the capacity of a crane. If out of level, there is possible capacity loss. The table below demonstrates this relationship for a particular crane.

Similar information can be obtained from the manufacturers for all cranes. Machines that are used on barges are provided with "list charts" that identify crane capacity with barge list (expressed as degrees). Capacity loss due to barge list is the same as capacity loss due to an out-of-level condition on ground.

Boom Length and Lift Radius	Chart Capacity Lost When Crane Out of Level By		
	1°	2°	3°
Short Boom, Minimum Radius	10%	20%	30%
Short Boom, Maximum Radius	8%	15%	20%
Long Boom, Minimum Radius	30%	41%	50%
Long Boom, Maximum Radius	5%	10%	15%

Crane Not Level (continued)

> **Caution:** If the crane is not level the load chart does not apply. You must either level the crane by using its outriggers or level the ground the machine is resting on.
> Even though the crane might have been properly levelled during set-up, ground subsidence during operation can cause an out-of-level condition. Check level frequently.

It is also important to note that when a crane is set up off level, swinging from the high side to the low side increases the operating radius. It also increases the load on the turntable, on the outriggers and on the supporting frame structure.

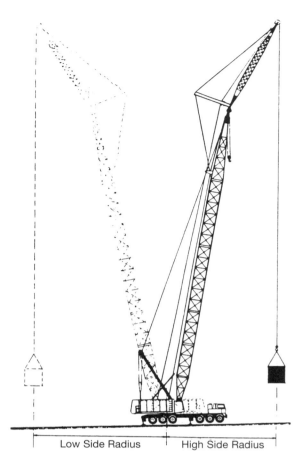

Low Side Radius   High Side Radius

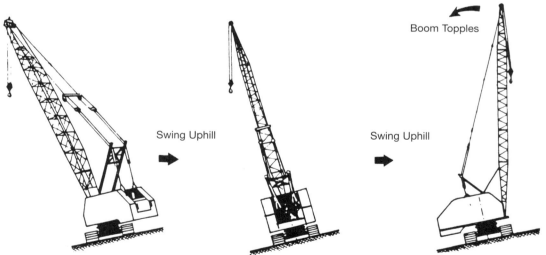

Boom Topples

Swing Uphill   Swing Uphill

Caution: A boom at maximum elevation (minimum radius) on the low side cannot be swung over to the high side without risking collapse of the boom over the cab.

Sideloading

Load chart ratings apply only when the load is picked up directly under the boom tip. If the load is to either side of the boom tip, sideloading occurs and decreases capacity. This applies to both lattice and telescopic booms and is one of the most common causes of boom failure. It usually causes structural failure and always occurs without warning.

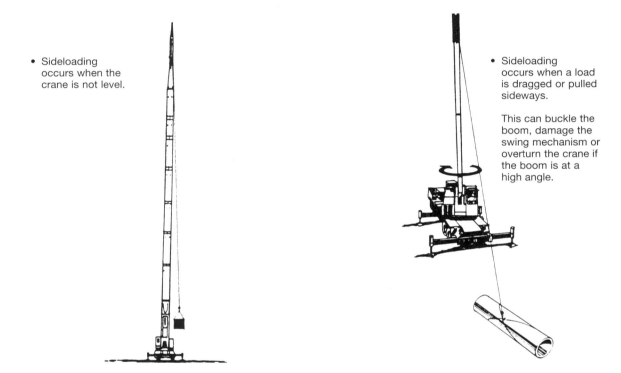

- Sideloading occurs when the crane is not level.

- Sideloading occurs when a load is dragged or pulled sideways.

  This can buckle the boom, damage the swing mechanism or overturn the crane if the boom is at a high angle.

Sideloading (continued)

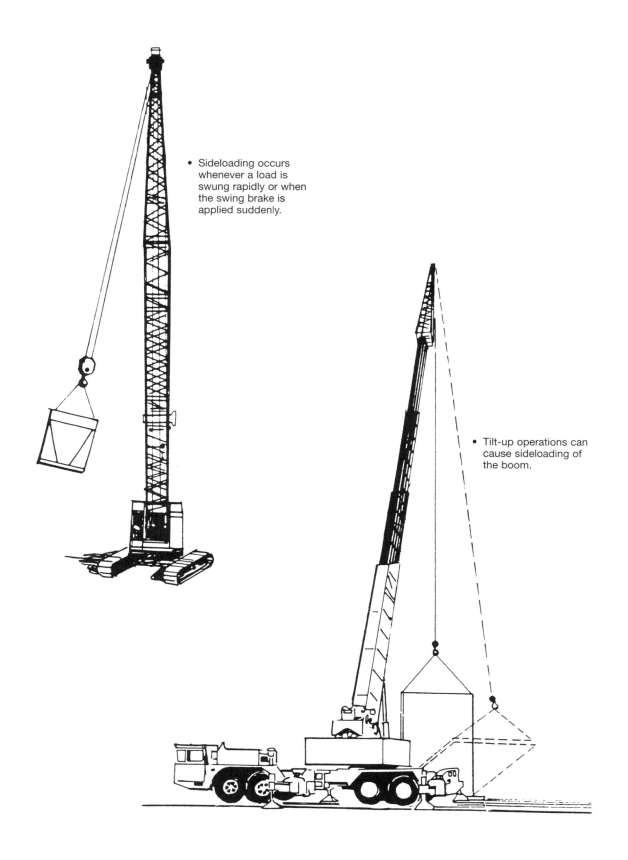

- Sideloading occurs whenever a load is swung rapidly or when the swing brake is applied suddenly.

- Tilt-up operations can cause sideloading of the boom.

Increase of Load Radius

Load chart ratings apply only when the hoist line is vertical at all times and the load is freely suspended during the lift. If the line is not vertical, regardless of the reasons, capacity is lost. In addition to the examples relating to sideloading (see previous pages), the following conditions produce non-vertical hoist lines which result in increased load radius and reduced capacity.

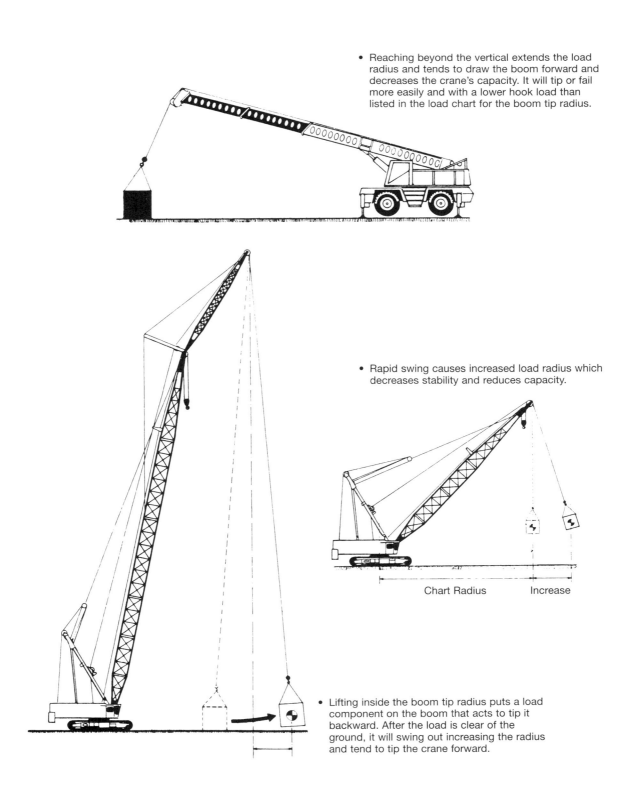

- Reaching beyond the vertical extends the load radius and tends to draw the boom forward and decreases the crane's capacity. It will tip or fail more easily and with a lower hook load than listed in the load chart for the boom tip radius.

- Rapid swing causes increased load radius which decreases stability and reduces capacity.

Chart Radius   Increase

- Lifting inside the boom tip radius puts a load component on the boom that acts to tip it backward. After the load is clear of the ground, it will swing out increasing the radius and tend to tip the crane forward.

Increase of Load Radius (continued)

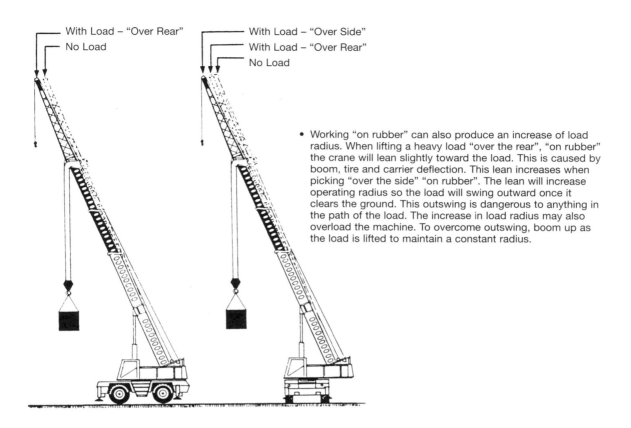

With Load – "Over Rear"
No Load

With Load – "Over Side"
With Load – "Over Rear"
No Load

• Working "on rubber" can also produce an increase of load radius. When lifting a heavy load "over the rear", "on rubber" the crane will lean slightly toward the load. This is caused by boom, tire and carrier deflection. This lean increases when picking "over the side" "on rubber". The lean will increase operating radius so the load will swing outward once it clears the ground. This outswing is dangerous to anything in the path of the load. The increase in load radius may also overload the machine. To overcome outswing, boom up as the load is lifted to maintain a constant radius.

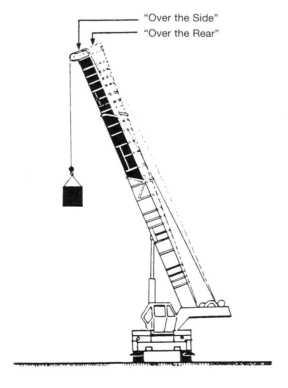

"Over the Side"
"Over the Rear"

• Swinging a load from "over the end" to "over the side" will increase lean. This is especially noticeable when operating "on tires". Since tilt acts to increase load radius, it must be compensated for when swinging the load. Swing slowly. Change boom angle (raise or lower boom) while swinging to maintain a constant radius and prevent inswing or outswing of load.

Rapid Swing Rate

Load chart ratings apply only when the load is vertically in line with the boom tip at all times. Rapid swing rates make this an impossible condition to meet.

Therefore, load chart capacities do not allow for fast swings. The swing rate must be adjusted to keep the load directly below the boom tip at all times.

(1) START SWING   **(2) DURING SWING**   **(3) STOP SWING**

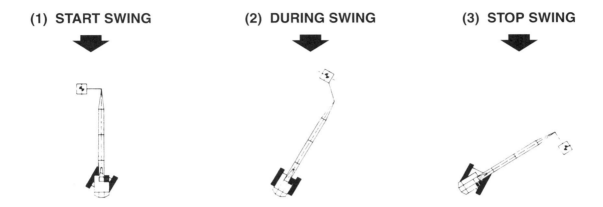

(1) When the swing is started the load will lag behind the boom tip causing sideloading and reducing capacity.

(2) Rapid swinging of a load causes it to drift away from the machine increasing the load radius and reducing capacity; the load will also lag behind the boom tip causing sideloading.

(3) When the crane's swing is stopped, the load will keep going causing sideloading and reducing capacity.

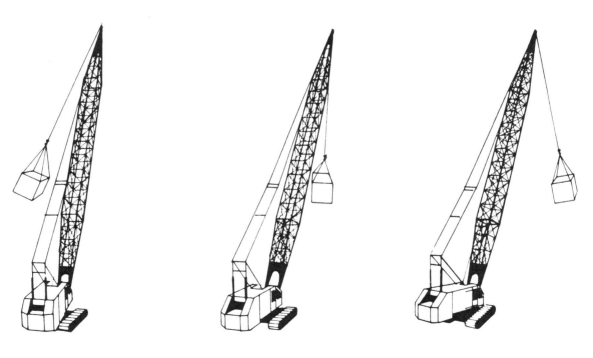

> **Caution:** On long boom mobile cranes, rapid swing rates, rapid swing acceleration, or rapid application of the swing brake can overturn the crane or collapse the boom *with or without load on the hook.*

- Moving the dead weight of the boom at the start of a swing or trying to stop it at the end of a swing causes the boom to sideload itself.

- The centrifugal force of the boom during a high speed swing creates a high forward tipping load.

- At high boom angles, the boom can collapse over the back of the machine if the boom is accelerated or decelerated rapidly.

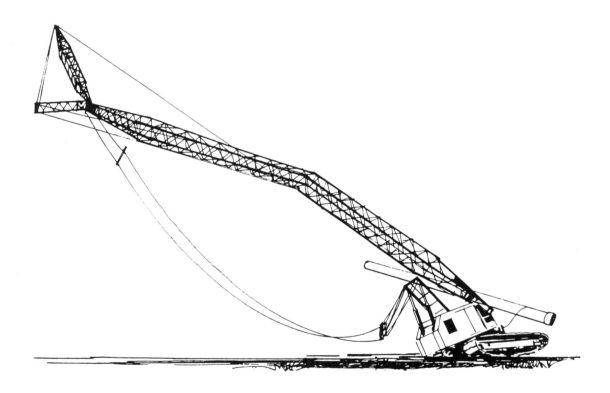

Impact Loading and Rapid Acceleration or Deceleration of Load

Load chart capacities do not allow for sudden starting or stopping of the load, impact loading or sudden machine movements.

The following situations create such conditions and reduce crane capacity below the chart ratings.

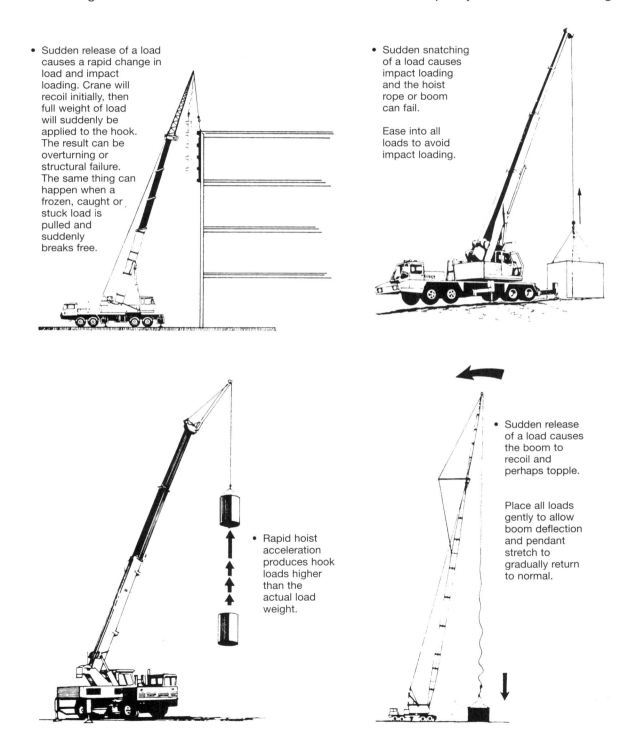

- Sudden release of a load causes a rapid change in load and impact loading. Crane will recoil initially, then full weight of load will suddenly be applied to the hook. The result can be overturning or structural failure. The same thing can happen when a frozen, caught or stuck load is pulled and suddenly breaks free.

- Sudden snatching of a load causes impact loading and the hoist rope or boom can fail.

  Ease into all loads to avoid impact loading.

- Rapid hoist acceleration produces hook loads higher than the actual load weight.

- Sudden release of a load causes the boom to recoil and perhaps topple.

  Place all loads gently to allow boom deflection and pendant stretch to gradually return to normal.

Impact Loading and Rapid Acceleration or Deceleration of Load (continued)

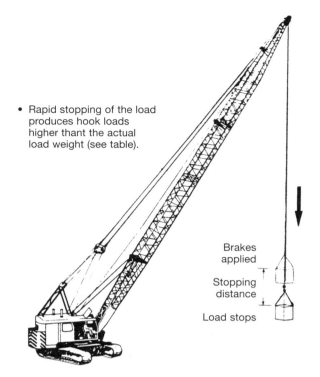

- Rapid stopping of the load produces hook loads higher thant the actual load weight (see table).

Brakes applied

Stopping distance

Load stops

- "Pick and Carry" operations subject the carrier and boom to shock loads. In order to ensure that the chart capacities are not exceeded, move the crane and load as smoothly as possible.

Sudden brake application during lowering will increase the hook load. Below is an example of how line speed and stopping distance impact the load on the hook. Note how rapidly the loads increase as the stopping distance decreases.

INCREASE IN HOOK LOADS

LINE SPEED FT/MIN.	STOPPING DISTANCE (FT)		
	10	6	2
100	0.4%	0.7%	2.2%
150	1.0%	1.6%	4.9%
200	1.7%	2.9%	8.6%
250	2.7%	4.5%	13.5%
300	3.9%	6.5%	19.4%
350	5.3%	8.8%	26.4%
400	6.9%	11.5%	34.5%

- Don't extract pilings, casings or similar loads by yanking or jerking on them. The practice of pulling on the load until the machine has tipped, then releasing the hoist line, allowing the machine to drop back and catching the hoist line on a clutch or brake may break the boom. If the piling or casing won't dislodge with a smooth, steady pull, use an extractor, pulling frame or similar device.

- Demolition work can be particularly hazardous. Shock loadings and sideloadings during work with demolition balls and clamshell buckets can be severe. The repetitive nature of such work imposes heavy demands on all parts of the machine. Restrict demolition ball weights to not more than 50% of capacity ("on rubber" capacities for truck cranes) at the maximum radius at which you handle the ball, with the boom length you are using. In addition to this requirement, ensure that the ball weight never exceeds 50% of the available line pull.

Duty Cycle Operations

Full load chart ratings may not apply when cranes are used in high speed production operations (duty cycle operations) such as concrete placing, steel erection, draglining, clam, magnet or grapple work.

The manufacturer will either specify in the load chart that lift crane ratings be reduced by a percentage (usually 20%) for duty cycle operations or will supply a separate load chart for such operations.

The capacity reduction is recommended because the speed of these operations produces increases in crane loads from sideload, swing-out and impact as well as higher temperatures in critical components such as brakes, clutches, pumps and motors.

The following are duty cycle operations:

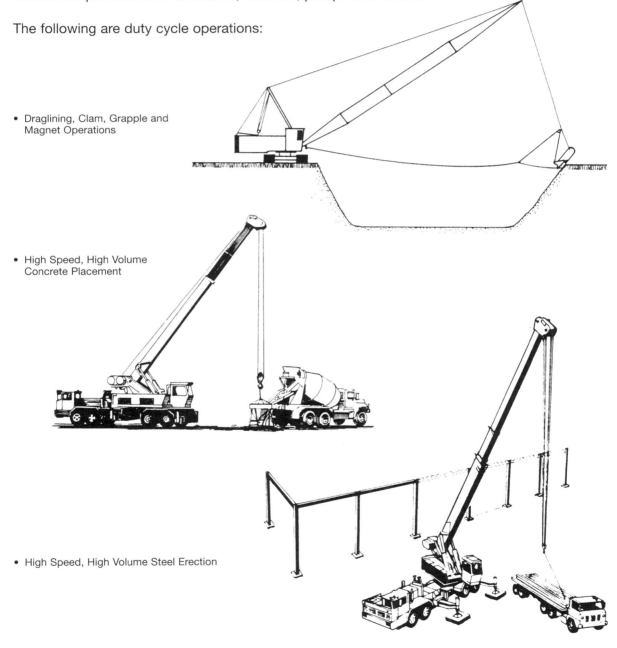

- Draglining, Clam, Grapple and
  Magnet Operations

- High Speed, High Volume
  Concrete Placement

- High Speed, High Volume Steel Erection

High Wind Speeds

Almost all crane manufacturers specify in the load chart that chart ratings must be reduced under windy conditions, and they may also recommend a shut-down wind velocity. In almost all cases, when the wind speed exceeds *30 mph,* it is advisable to *stop* operations.

Wind affects both the crane and the load, reducing the rated capacity of the crane. Never make a full capacity lift if it is windy. Use a great deal of discretion even when lifting under moderate wind conditions of 20 mph.

It is advisable to avoid handling loads that present large wind-catching surfaces. The result could be loss of control of the load and crane even though the weight of the load is within the normal capacity of the crane.

A 20 mph wind exerts a force of only 1⅛ lb/ft^2 on a flat-surfaced load (the force on a 4 ft. by 8 ft. sheet of plywood = 36 lbs.) so only loads having very large sail areas would require crane capacity derating. At 30 mph, however, the wind exerts a force of 2.53 lb/ft^2 of flat surface area (equals 80 lbs. on a sheet of 4 ft. by 8 ft. plywood). This wind force on the load at 30 mph is enough to cause non-vertical hoist lines and loads that are very difficult to control.

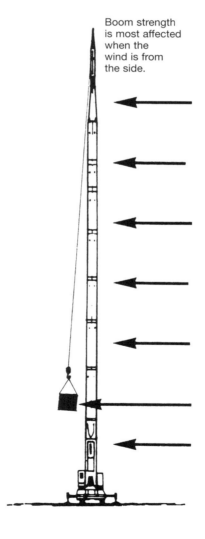

Boom strength is most affected when the wind is from the side.

SAE XJ1093 specifies that booms be designed to withstand their full rated load <u>plus</u> a side load equal to 2% of the rated load <u>plus</u> a 20 mph wind from the side. Boom strength is therefore adequate to handle winds from the side up to 20 mph <u>but</u> no allowance is made for the effect of the wind on the load.

Setup Summary

A crane is properly set up for lifting when the following conditions are met.

For Cranes Operating "On Outriggers"

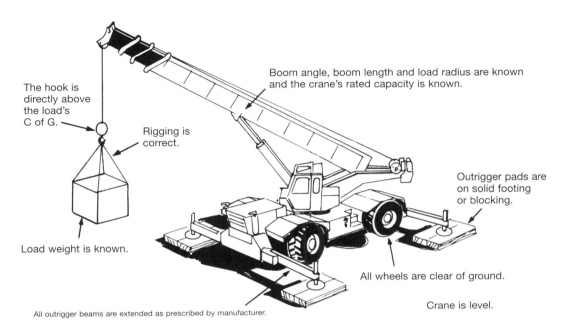

The hook is directly above the load's C of G.

Rigging is correct.

Boom angle, boom length and load radius are known and the crane's rated capacity is known.

Outrigger pads are on solid footing or blocking.

Load weight is known.

All wheels are clear of ground.

Crane is level.

All outrigger beams are extended as prescribed by manufacturer.

For Crawler-Mounted Cranes or When Lifting "On Rubber"

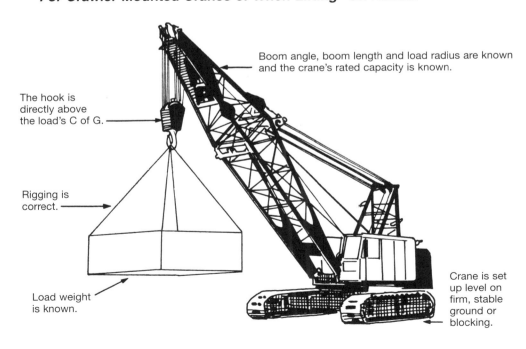

The hook is directly above the load's C of G.

Boom angle, boom length and load radius are known and the crane's rated capacity is known.

Rigging is correct.

Load weight is known.

Crane is set up level on firm, stable ground or blocking.

Machine Selection

One basic requirement for any crane safety program is making sure that the right machine is selected for the job. If crane characteristics do not match job requirements, unsafe conditions are created before any work is done. Job site personnel are forced to "make do" and improvise in a rush – a surefire recipe for accidents

---

CHECKPOINTS

No machine should be selected to do any lifting on a specific job until its size and characteristics are considered against:

- the weights, dimensions, and lift radii of the heaviest and largest loads
- the maximum lift height, the maximum lift radius, and the weight of the loads that must be handled at each
- the number and frequency of lifts to be made
- how long the crane will be required on site
- the type of lifting to be done (for example, is precision placement of loads important?)
- the type of carrier required (this depends on ground conditions and machine capacity in its various operating quadrants: capacity is normally greatest over the rear, less over the side, and non-existent over the front)
- whether loads will have to be walked or carried
- whether loads will have to be suspended for lengthy periods
- the site conditions, including the ground where the machine will be set up, access roads and ramps it must travel, space for erection, and any obstacles that might impede access or operation service availability and unit cost
- the cost of operations such as erection, dismantling, on- and off-site transport, and altering boom length.

RESULTS

The selected machine should:

- be able to make all of its lifts in its standard configuration (that means having the capacity and boom length to do all known tasks, with jib, extra counterweight, and special reeving held in reserve for any unexpected problems)

- have at least a 5% working margin with respect to the load capacity of every lift

- be highly mobile and capable of being routed with a minimum amount of tearing down

- have enough clearance between load and boom and adequate head room between the load and whatever rigging is required to make the lift.

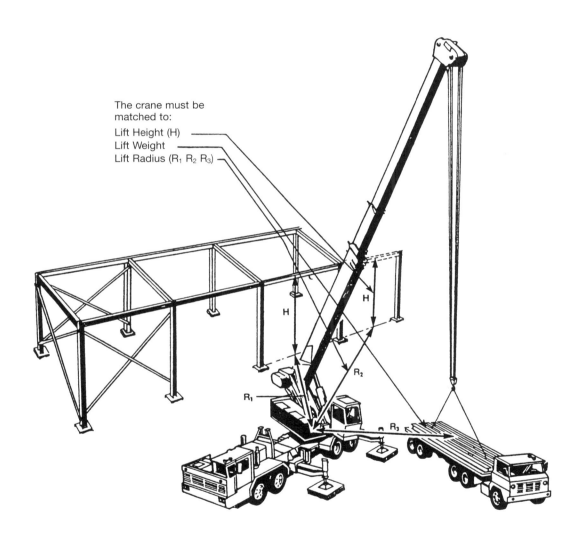

The crane must be matched to:
Lift Height (H)
Lift Weight
Lift Radius (R_1 R_2 R_3)

THE CRANE MUST BE PROPERLY MATCHED TO THE JOB

Those responsible for equipment selection must ensure that the crane is going to be safe and reliable for as long as it will be used, and under all anticipated conditions to which it will be exposed during operation.

Certain equipment considerations and requirements apply to all cranes. These requirements can be specified in purchase orders and rental agreements. Machines should be rented only from reputable suppliers. Note that all cranes of the same model number may not have the same capacity rating. The correct rating should be determined from the manufacturer through the serial number.

Any changes in counterweight and boom inserts made by the owner should be checked. After such changes, capacities and other data in the load chart may no longer apply.

A machine designed, manufactured, inspected, tested, and maintained in accordance with Canadian Standards Association *Standard Z150-1998 Mobile Cranes* should meet the requirements of all major codes and regulations.

Signalling

Signalling is an important part of crane operation, but is often not treated with the respect it deserves. Signallers must be used whenever:

- the operator cannot see the load
- the operator cannot see the load's landing area
- the operator cannot see the path of travel of the load or of the crane
- the operator is far enough away from the load to make the judgment of distance difficult
- the crane is working within a boom's length of the approach limits to powerlines or electrical equipment.

Where loads are picked up at one point and lowered at another, two signallers may be required – one to direct the lift and one to direct the descent.

Hand signals should be used only when the distance between the operator and the signaller is not great and conditions allow for clear visibility. The international hand signals for hoisting appear on the following page.

Telephone or radio communications between operator and signaller can be extremely effective.

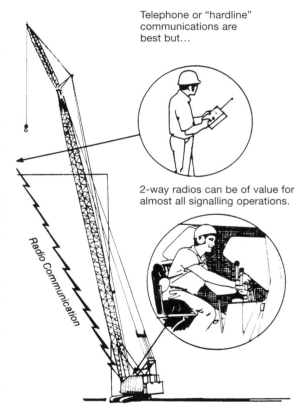

Telephone or "hardline" communications are best but...

2-way radios can be of value for almost all signalling operations.

Radio Communication

HOISTING HAND SIGNALS

Notes